Engaging Classrooms and Communities through Art

Engaging Classrooms and Communities through Art

A Guide to Designing and Implementing Community-Based Art Education

Beth Krensky
and
Seana Lowe Steffen

AltaMira Press
A Division of
ROWMAN & LITTLEFIELD PUBLISHERS, INC.
Lanham • Boulder • New York • Toronto • Plymouth, UK

ALTAMIRA PRESS
A division of Rowman & Littlefield Publishers, Inc.
A wholly owned subsidiary of The Rowman & Littlefield Publishing Group, Inc.
4501 Forbes Boulevard, Suite 200
Lanham, MD 20706
www.altamirapress.com

Estover Road
Plymouth PL6 7PY
United Kingdom

British Library Cataloguing in Publication Information Available

Library of Congress Cataloguing-in-Publication Data

Krensky, Beth, 1965–
Engaging classrooms and communities through art : a guide to designing and implementing community-based art education / Beth Krensky and Seana Lowe Steffen.
p. cm.
ISBN-13: 978-0-7591-1067-0 (cloth : alk. paper)
ISBN-10: 0-7591-1067-0 (cloth : alk. paper)
ISBN-13: 978-0-7591-1068-7 (pbk. : alk. paper)
ISBN-10: 0-7591-1068-9 (pbk. : alk. paper)
ISBN-13: 978-0-7591-1233-9 (electronic)
ISBN-10: 0-7591-1233-9 (electronic)
1. Community arts projects—United States. 2. Arts—Study and teaching—United States. I. Steffen, Seana Lowe. II. Title.

NX180.A77K74 2009
700.71'073—dc22 2008022200

Printed in the United States of America

∞™ The paper used in this publication meets the minimum requirements of American National Standard for Information Sciences—Permanence of Paper for Printed Library Materials, ANSI/NISO Z39.48-1992.

This book is dedicated to Deloris Ann Case, whose artistic and playful spirit so lovingly nurtured my creative self.

Seana Lowe Steffen

This book is dedicated to Celia June Goldner Hozid, who paved a path for me to walk down to become a scholar, and to the amazing young artists from Boston and Colorado who have been my greatest teachers.

Beth Krensky

Contents

The Theory and Practice of Community Art

Foreword

In 1980 I was recruited straight out of college to begin teaching art to special education middle school students in a public school on Kelly Street in the South Bronx. Back then, the South Bronx was on fire, literally. Simply walking down Prospect Avenue—one of the neighborhood's once-grand boulevards—was an assault on the mind and senses. The air was acrid with the odor of burned tenement buildings, and the wind wheezed as it blew through their charred and gutted shells. Coming from rural central Maine, I had never in my life or imagination been placed in such a distressed, struggling, and impossible landscape. How could people be expected to live here, let alone learn?

But after weeks, months, and eventually years as an artist and educator in the neighborhood, I began to discover that the South Bronx was also on fire culturally. The music, fashion, food, murals, and many fine works of public art by such artists as Rafael Ferrer, Michael Kelly Williams, and John Ahearn were everywhere. Out of the ashes of the place, the entire community beamed with promise and hope. I would wager that the area was developing more vernacular and fine art than one would encounter in any other neighborhood in the nation. The South Bronx surely has had its heroes, and they are the artists—the painters, writers, photographers, cartoonists, animators, graffiti artists, fashion designers, musicians, singers, dancers, poets, and filmmakers.

In 1984, armed with a small grant from the National Endowment for the Arts, a group of my most devoted arts students and I were able to establish a working fine arts studio—the Art and Knowledge Workshop—in an abandoned elementary school gymnasium in the neighborhood. Calling themselves "K.O.S." ("Kids of Survival"), my students collaborated with me on large-scale paintings inspired by themes drawn from world literature and music. Together we began engaging with the writing, themes, and ethos of such books as Hawthorne's *The Scarlet Letter*, Kafka's *Amerika*, and Ralph Ellison's *Invisible Man*. We searched these great novels for the language, issues, and relevance their stories might have for our everyday lives, allowing us to create visual correspondences in our paintings. In the creation of each new artwork, a rigorous and often-surprising curriculum involving language arts, art and global history, philosophy, ethics, mathematics, aesthetics, and craft was organically generated.

After twenty-five years of work, the long-term results of our collaboration are encouraging, even celebratory. Our paintings are currently in the permanent collections of more than eighty-five museums, including The Museum of Modern Art in New York, the Hirshhorn Museum in Washington, D.C., and the Tate Modern in London. While we continue to live and work close to our South Bronx roots, we also orchestrate artworks and workshops with struggling communities across the United States and internationally. I feel our greatest collective achievements have been the numbers of K.O.S. members who made their way to colleges and universities like Bard College, the University of Pennsylvania, the School of Visual Arts, San Francisco Art Institute, and Stanford University. Like the lives of these young artists, the South Bronx has been rebuilt, restored, and resurrected, primarily through the power of its arts in concert with grassroots community organizations, churches, and government initiatives.

After this life experience as an art educator in the Bronx, I am personally and professionally excited by the appearance of Beth Krensky and Seana Lowe Steffen's *Engaging Classrooms and Communities through Art*. Community artists, and especially those folks who are intrigued and enthusiastic about beginning this work, have been in dire need of such a guide for a long time. While most publications about community-based art have documented or described the successes and failures of already-existing projects, Krensky and Steffen actually provide information and inspiration for implementing and sustaining excellent community arts practices. The past, present, and future of this work require such a "how-to" book, especially now, when the number of community-based arts initiatives is exploding worldwide. How do we get started? How do we sustain our energies? How do we define community? What are the immediate and long-term effects on the lives of the participants and the communities they come from? These are a few of the constantly challenging questions that *Engaging Classrooms and Communities through Art* addresses in practical and useful terms.

Work with my community has taught me that through the transformative power of art, even negative experiences can offer gravity, grace, and authenticity, resulting in powerful works of art. Through the restorative power of community-based art making, the often-indescribable joy of living and pressing on can be shared to inspire the aspirations of others. For many communities, art is simply vision made visible and hope made manifest. I am grateful that Krensky and Steffen's book supports and replicates this testimony.

Professor Tim Rollins

Biographical Note

Professor Tim Rollins is the founder of the Art and Knowledge Workshop and K.O.S. in the South Bronx. Rollins has also been a Distinguished Professor at the University of California, Davis; a Resident Professor at Drexel University; and a Visiting Professor at the University of Virginia and the Cooper Union. Rollins is currently a Professor of Fine Art at the School of Visual Arts in New York City and a Visiting Professor of Art, Literature, and Music at the Martha Washington Elementary School in West Philadelphia. Rollins resides in the Longwood neighborhood in the South Bronx.

Acknowledgments

*This book was equally authored by Beth Krensky and Seana Lowe Steffen.

In keeping with the nature of community art, this book was a co-creation that involved many generous contributions from members of our community. We would like to thank the organizations and individuals from our research sites that gave their time and shared their experiences to provide the data on which this book is based. We also would like to thank those individuals who contributed portions of this book: Jennifer Atkinson, Juliet Biagi, Matt Bradley, Kathleen Kingsley, Deborah Reshotko, Tim Rollins, and Irina Zadov. In addition, we are grateful to such organizations as Boys & Girls Clubs of Boston, Charlestown Club; Neighborhood Cultures of Denver; Project YES; SPEAKING OF DANCE; and Spy Hop Productions, all of which engage in the important service of bringing community-based art education to the world. We extend special acknowledgment to those people whose support has assisted us through the final stages of this process, including Juliet Biagi for her brilliant editorial contributions and insights, and Jamie Rezmovits for her work as the book's artistic editor. Finally, we thank our editors Serena Krombach and Christopher Anzalone at AltaMira Press for their belief in and support of this project, as well as Krista Sprecher and Marissa Marro for their outstanding effort.

Beth Krensky and Seana Lowe Steffen

My belief in humanity's creative capacity to transform our world inspires me to be a community sociologist. I teach community leadership. I benefit from the power of intentional community to enhance the quality of my life daily. And, like so many of the most meaningful and most significant things worth doing in life, the opportunity to write this book was blessed by the special people in my community who partnered with me.

There were many who provided guidance and support during the journey of creating this book. I offer my gratitude to my mentors Dr. Jim Downton and Dr. Marki LeCompte. Jim, thank you for having faith in me and for encouraging me to choose an authentic and balanced path. Your compassionate guidance and gifts of woo wisdom brought color to my creative process. Marki, thank you for your rigor and your willingness to live a professional life that has integrity. Your theoretical and methodological expertise significantly transformed the quality of my work. I also want to thank Juliet Biagi: your creative vision inspired the multimedia park project. Learning and serving with you was such a joy. And to my dear friend Dr. Beth Krensky, artist–activist–educator extraordinaire, thank you for the coffee talks and morning walks and vigorous belief in what is possible for the world. I would never have remembered my love for the arts or experienced my creative potential were it not for your inspiration. I honor you tremendously. Thank you for being my treasured colleague and friend.

I also want to thank my family. To my parents, Jana Lowe and Richard Lowe, who taught me to believe in myself and to believe that anything is possible, thank you for giving me life and access to a life that I love. I am so blessed to be your daughter. To my dear friend Jamie, thank you for your love and support during the difficult life circumstances that paralleled this journey. You are the embodiment of generosity and thoughtfulness. And thank you to my Lunessence community of women guides who have taught me the power of community to heal and to transform.

Last, and primary in my life, thank you to my husband, Barron Steffen—you are my muse. Thank you for being an unwavering stand for my well-being. You have inspired me to be my best self by bringing out the best in others with your goodness and light. I am so grateful to the universe for aligning our paths as twin souls: "so intimate that when I fall asleep it is your eyes that close." My love for you is eternal.

Seana Lowe Steffen

I would like to gratefully thank the following people whose vision and guidance have shaped this work and nourished me during the process. First, my sincere thanks to the young people from the Boys & Girls Clubs of Boston, Charlestown Club; Project YES; and Lafayette, Colorado, for being my teachers and for daring to dream; to Juliet Biagi, for having endless creativity and being an exemplary leader; to Jamie Rezmovits, who supported this work in the early stages by lovingly watching Zev; to Dr. Michele Moses, for years of ongoing support and inspiration; and to Dr. Carole MacNeil, for co-founding Project YES and co-creating the Project YES curriculum, which is a foundation for much of the work described in this book, and for the years of friendship, conversation, and action—you have been a guiding force and inspiration for my work as an educator, artist, and scholar. Finally, I want to thank Dr. Seana Lowe Steffen for suggesting that we collectively write this manuscript, for unwavering encouragement, and for keeping the momentum alive so that we could co-create this book—you are an educator, scholar, and activist extraordinaire. I have cherished our time together as friends and colleagues.

I would like to thank my academic mentors for their support and encouragement and for being examples to me of committed scholars whose work makes a difference. In particular, I want to thank Dr. Margaret (Marki) LeCompte, who has been the greatest of mentors and has provided me with all of the tools I needed for this journey and beyond; Dr. George Rivera, whose passion for and commitment to art for social change have been an inspiration to me and impacted my work greatly; Dr. Gary Orfield, who believed in and supported the very formative stages of this work; and Dr. Dan Liston, Dr. Maria Franquiz, and Dr. Dick Kraft for their insightful guidance. I would also like to thank Dr. Stephanie Richardson, Dr. David Dynak, and the members of the Fine Arts Scholars group from the College of Fine Arts at the University of Utah for ongoing support and inspiration throughout the final writing stages of this manuscript.

I would like to thank my parents for teaching me the importance of using my time and abilities to make the world a better place. In particular, I want to thank my mother, Doris Hozid Krensky, for showing me the power and joy of being both a teacher and a learner. Your lifelong belief in *all* young people has influenced my path more than you will ever know.

I want to thank Zev Elijah Krensky Gorfinkle for simply being. My love for you has helped me understand how precious and important all children are everywhere.

Finally, I want to thank my beloved, Edward Gorfinkle, whose love and support have been steadfast throughout all of my endeavors. Your encouragement, laughter, technical assistance, and time spent keeping our home and lives in order made it possible for me to accomplish this work. I am deeply grateful for your generosity of both spirit and action.

Beth Krensky

SECTION ONE

UNDERSTANDING COMMUNITY ART

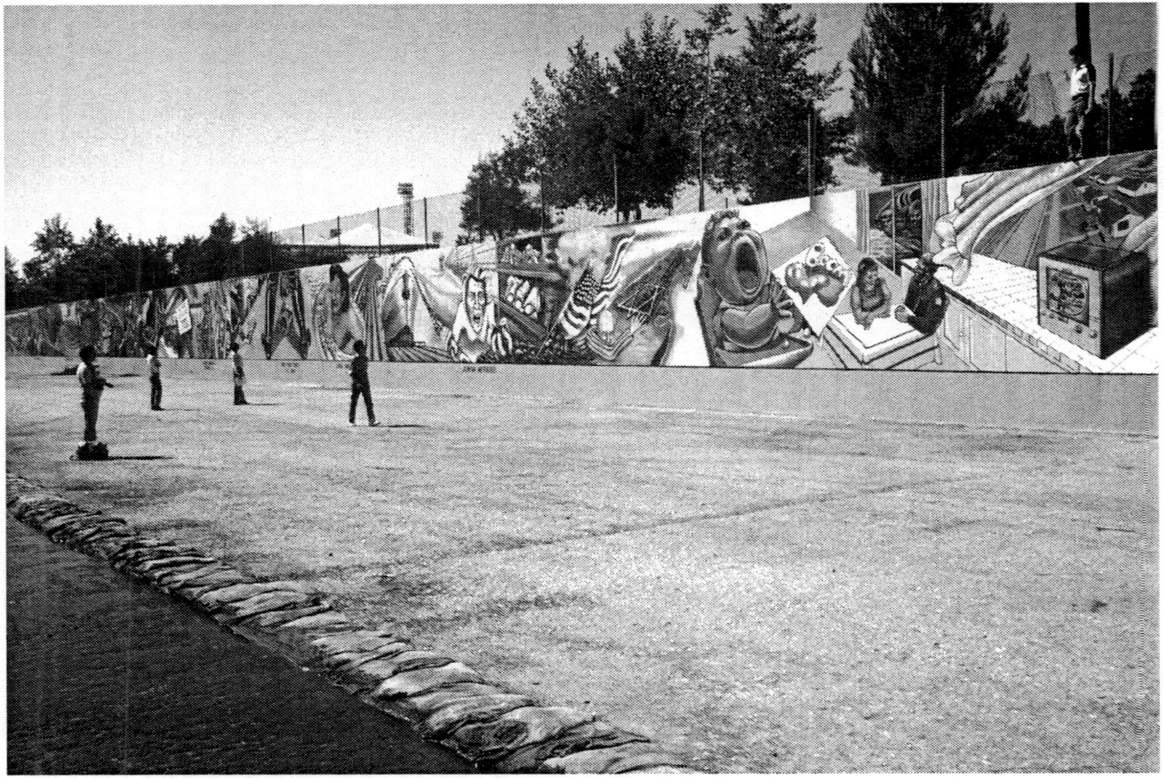

Figure 1.1. ***The Great Wall,* 1976–2001, Los Angeles, California, Judith Baca,** Community Art **Mural.**

CHAPTER ONE

Introduction to Community Art and Community-Based Art Education

We believe that the arts have a unique power to inspire us, as human beings, to see creative possibilities for our world and ourselves. Art connects us to our shared humanity and to our fundamental human need to create. This book is for those who value art for art's sake, for those who see its role as a means to extraordinary ends, and for those who believe that education should be renewing to our society and our lives. This book is for artists who seek art that is relevant and authentically connected to the lived experience of its makers and its viewers, for practitioners who value relationships and spaces beyond the classroom and studio, and for those who believe in the power of the arts to touch imagination, evoke possibility, and alter life.

The Power of the Arts

It is the nature of art to create openings where one can envision something outside the realm of what already exists for oneself, one's community, and the world—a realm where anything is possible. Artists and art practitioners know that it is within this free space for creative expression that people can explore new identities and possibilities for themselves and their communities, moving beyond perceptions of limiting boundaries and circumstances. As John Dewey articulated, changes in the imagination are the precursors to changes in society: "Only imaginative vision elicits the possibilities that are interwoven within the texture of the actual . . . the first intimations of a better future are always found in works of art."[1]

In spite of the perceived and proven value of the arts, fewer and fewer Americans are experiencing the transformative power of the arts during their education. Art programs in schools across the United States have been cut as education budgets diminish. At the time of this book's printing, only half of all elementary schools in the United States have full-time art teachers,[2] which means that many of our nation's youth are not receiving an adequate art education. When the resources, tools, and knowledge necessary to experience, express, and learn about oneself and one's world through the arts are not provided, critically important opportunities for personal and cultural expression are lost forever. This is a tremendous cost to individuals and to society.

Concurrent with the decline of arts funding and programming in schools, the arts have emerged quietly, yet significantly, to promote healthy communities and to augment prevention and intervention efforts in the independent and public sectors. In particular, the use of community art and community-based art education to build community and foster change has emerged as a striking trend in recent decades. At the federal level, the President's Committee on the Arts and the Humanities has highlighted the importance of the arts for underserved children. Two national studies, *Coming Up Taller: Arts and Humanities Programs for Children and Youth at Risk*[3] and *Part of the Solution: Creative Alternatives for Youth*,[4] found that community-art programs provide unique opportunities for youth to envision and actualize more positive futures for themselves and their communities. These programs are using the arts to "enrich, transform and even save lives. And in so doing they help to address some of society's greatest challenges, especially those involving youth."[5] Indeed, community art as community cultural development is being used to address issues ranging from culture wars to the environment.[6]

Effective examples of community-art programs can be found around the country. The Arts and Prevention partnership between the Center for Substance Abuse Prevention and the National Endowment for the Arts represents an effort to involve artists and art organizations in substance abuse prevention programs. The National Endowment for the Arts and other public and private foundations have been helping future generations realize their potential through creative expression by financing art projects with state and regional partners. At the state and local levels, such grassroots organizations as Project YES in Colorado are combining arts and service learning to inspire young people to take leadership roles in solving social problems. SPEAKING OF DANCE in Denver uses dance as a tool to bring diverse groups of people together to celebrate the joy and drama of being human while simultaneously examining social issues. In Utah, YouthCity Artways (formerly Global Artways) provides art experiences to youth and families in an effort to enhance physical, intellectual, emotional, and social development through arts enrichment and arts education. Spy Hop Productions also calls Utah home but works with youth from across the United States to engage them in film and video production, web design, and digital music to cultivate the visions and voices of an emerging generation.

Whether in schools or community-based organizations, these effective examples of using the arts for education, intervention, and prevention purposes are employing "those human activities that purposefully and qualitatively interpret, invent, extend and imbue meaning through organized visual form or enhance the form and meaning of objects. These activities are conceptualized as process and products of what we call art."[7] As reflections of living culture, works of art possess symbolic significance as well as transformative power for both individuals and communities. Art has the unique capacity to catalyze transformation because it inspires openings for creative possibilities on individual and societal levels as it satisfies fundamental human needs.

The arts play a unique and necessary role in fulfilling fundamental human needs that, when left unmet, jeopardize both individual and societal well-being. According to social psychologist Erich Fromm:

> Man [*sic*], in order to feel at home in the world, must grasp it not only with his head, but with all his senses, his eyes, his ears, with all his body. . . . If man [*sic*] expresses his grasp of the world by his senses, he creates art and ritual, he creates song, dance, drama, painting, sculpture. Collective art . . . is an integral part of life. It corresponds to a basic human need and if this need is not fulfilled, man [*sic*] remains as insecure and anxious as if the need for a meaningful thought picture of the world were unrealized. . . . No sane society can be built upon the mixture of purely intellectual knowledge and almost complete absence of shared artistic experience.[8]

Psychological research provides evidence of the critical importance of art and its capacity to mediate between people and their worlds. The arts play a role as the center "of biological and social individual processes in society, . . . a method for finding an equilibrium between man [*sic*] and his world, in the most critical and important stages of his life."[9] Art contains the essence of our humanity and "is the social technique of emotion, a tool of society which brings the most intimate and personal aspects of our being into the circle of social life. . . . Art is the social within us."[10] In anthropological circles, art also is considered essential to human survival because of its role in sustaining tradition and inspiring adaptation to change.[11]

Community Art and Community-Based Art Education

Given its power, art has been part of community life as a form of personal and cultural expression since the beginning of recorded history. A survey of the field suggests that three predominant social frameworks for the arts have emerged over time: civilizing, romantic, and transformative.[12] While the civilizing view regards art as an important factor in socializing appropriate norms and qualities for human and societal welfare, the romantic view sees the arts as "the expression of emotion through inspiration that leads to self-discovery and self-definition."[13] The transformative view integrates and expands the civilizing and romantic perspectives with a notion "that development of the imagination is the impetus for social change."[14] Thus, transformative arts explore, express, and emote in ways that inspire new possibilities for individuals and societies. For example, transformative arts can be used to redefine the self, build community, and address civic issues.

There are several different approaches to transformative art, including *public art*, *activist art*, and *community art*. According to David Fisher, *public art* is the display or performance of art in a public setting by a professional artist or artists.[15] In addition to inspiring aesthetic experiences, public art may fulfill a variety of functional, historical, and architectural purposes, as exemplified by many Works Progress Administration (WPA) projects that focused on "unifying art with everyday life"[16] during President Roosevelt's tenure. Maya Lin's *Vietnam Veterans Memorial* in Washington, D.C., and the *Chicago Picasso* are well-recognized examples of public art. While public art can be transformative, it is not inherently so.

Activist art also occurs in public settings, but in activist art, professional artists use this public display to address social and political issues and effect social change by engaging public interaction. Activist art is therefore, by definition, inherently transformative. According to Nina Felshin, activist art has three guiding characteristics: it must have political content, be created or displayed in public (not in museums or galleries), and create some interchange or interaction with the public.[17] While it may be argued that art has been used as a tool for social commentary and change throughout history, activist art as a creative endeavor has emerged specifically to "give voice and visibility to the disenfranchised and to connect art to a wider audience."[18] This new role of art is based on interaction, is context dependent, and is antihegemonic in that it broadens the definition of who may be an artist and what constitutes art. We expand Felshin's characteristics of activist art to allow for display in publicly accessible museums or galleries because of the change potential wielded by bringing disenfranchised perspectives to privileged audiences through traditional structures.

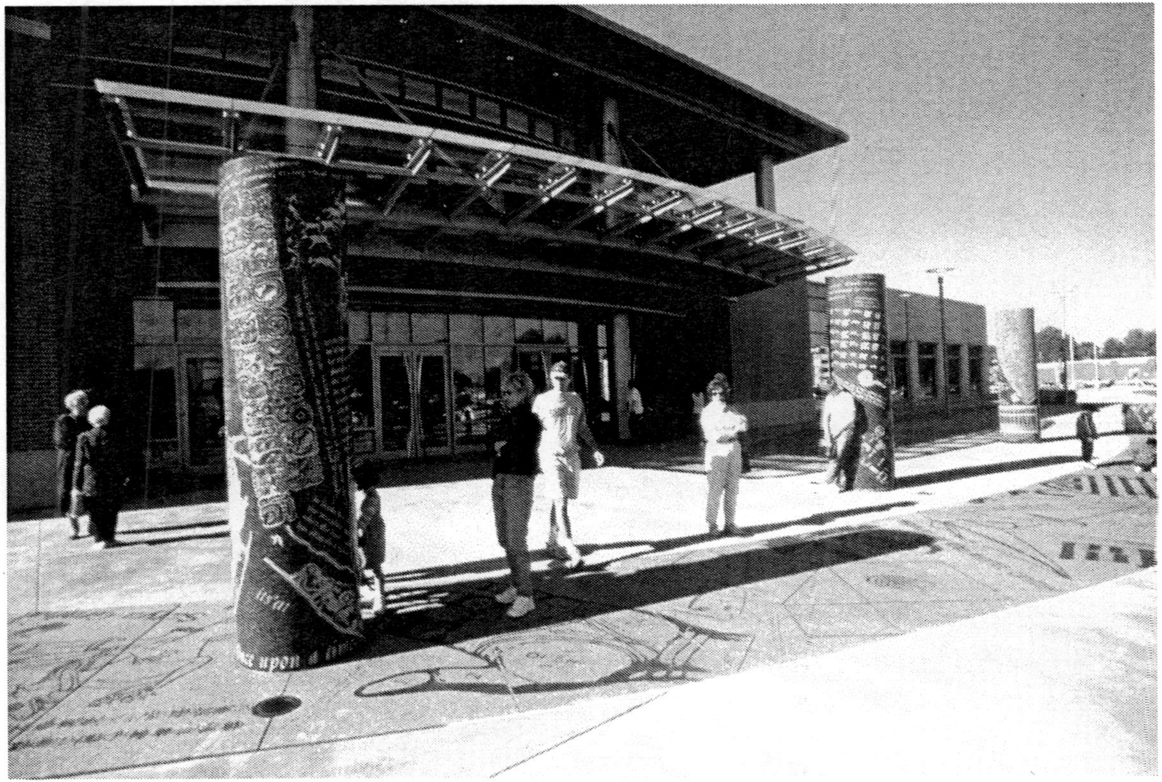

Figure 1.2. ***Explicitus Est Liber,*** **2002, Approx. 5,000 square feet, Garrison Roots,** Public Art **Memphis, Tenessee, Granite.**

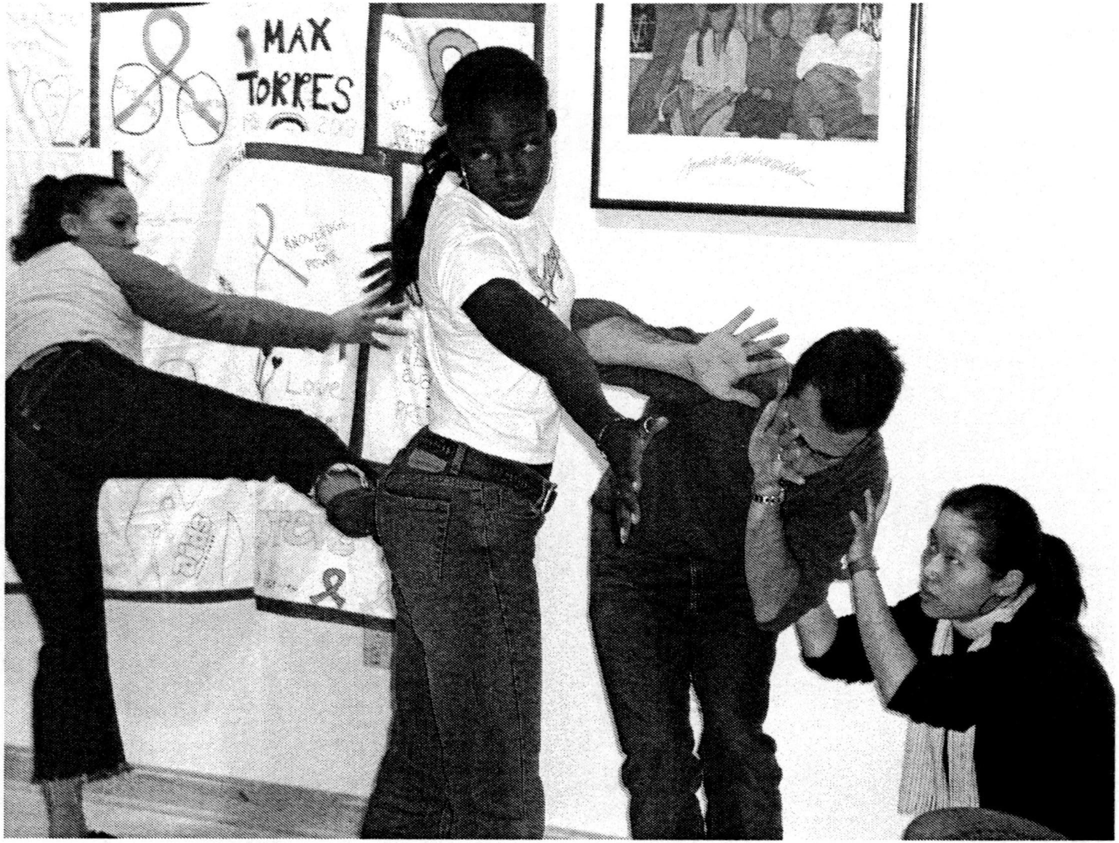

Figure 1.3. ***Interactive Theatre Performance*, 2004, Interactive Theater Project,** Activist Art, **Boulder, Colorado.**
Photo Credit: Karen Schuster

Individual artists, artist groups, and art programs use performances, exhibits, media events, and mainstream media to communicate their activist messages. For example, as a result of his anger and despair over the injustice of poverty, Augusto Boal was compelled to design art to serve educational, social, and therapeutic needs relating to all issues of oppression. His Brazilian *Theater of the Oppressed* serves as a precursor to action by using "physical exercises, aesthetic games, image techniques and special improvisations" to inspire actors and non-actors to understand and solve social problems.[19] In the United States, the *Guerrilla Girls* was founded in 1985 in response to frustration about sexism in the art world. To raise consciousness about progressive issues, the group's female artists wear gorilla masks and use humorous posters and performances to critique power structures and to provoke debate.[20] As an activist artist who uses photography to raise consciousness, Mev Puleo explains the rationale for his choice:

> Images can anesthetize, but they can also agitate and motivate. Photographs can manipulate reality or help name it. Pictures can distance us from one another or help us connect with each other. Art can be used as propaganda to indoctrinate, but it can also be a tool of advocacy for the dominated. . . . When we are aware that we do not take neutral photographs of the world, we can consciously choose to take photographs *for* the world we desire.[21]

Sama Alshaibi and Beth Krensky use photography and sculpture to foster the world of peace and reconciliation that they desire for their children. As Palestinian and Jewish women and mothers, their exhibition *We Make the Road by Walking* comes from a line by the Spanish poet Antonio Machado: "Se hace camino al andar," or "You can make the way as you go." At a time when the divide between Jews and Muslims remains ever challenging, their exhibit attempts to create a progressive dialogue between the two rich traditions of Islam and Judaism in America. The artists provide an important example of activist art framing civic dialogue.

Community art is similar to activist art by virtue of its experiential and inclusive nature. Community art is unique, however, because of its participatory design. With community art, professional artists work directly with others in grassroots settings to create art in the public interest.[22] For example, the community theater practices of the Philippine Educational Theater Association and The Netherlands' Stut Theater encourage and empower community participants to shape the content and form of their productions to authentically express messages about grassroots issues.[23]

Around the world, community art as a named phenomenon developed out of the activism of the 1960s and was intended to popularize art, returning it to the people.[24] Founders of the community arts movement believed in humanity's right to creative expression and in the importance of promoting creative expression for all people.[25] Community art is distinct from high art by its purpose and method:

> If community art is anything, it is the manifestation of an ideology. What makes it different from public art or art in the community, is its long-term cultural and political ambition. Whichever faction one belonged to in the seventies or eighties, there would be a number of points you could agree on, all revolving around the notion of empowerment through participation in the creative process. All community artists shared a dislike of cultural hierarchies, believed in co-authorship of work and in the creative potential of all sections of society. Some went further and believed that community arts provided a powerful medium for social and political change; . . . and working in the area of social and political issues, community arts could provide the blueprint for a truly participatory and egalitarian democracy.[26]

More expressly, community art is consistent with the beliefs:

> that everyone is an artist. . . . There is no doubt in the minds of community artists that social change takes place—for artists and community members alike . . . the production of art by people who don't define themselves as artists—is a radical, transformative act.[27]

Community art inherently results in social change by challenging the normative boundaries of the status hierarchy in the traditional art world through its collaborative art-making process. It uniquely brings the elite, cultural distinction of the professional artist together with lay people in the cultural activity of making art: "it resolves an ancient disunity by remarrying the artist and the populi."[28]

Community-Based Art Education

Community-based art education (CBAE) also places art in a community context.[29] In essence, CBAE is community art used as both a creative practice and a teaching method to fulfill educational objectives ranging from creative self-expression to competency with discipline-specific standards. This type of art education can sometimes be used for the purpose of social change by focusing the educational objectives on an exploration of social issues. In such cases, issue-oriented CBAE can be a tool to situate young people as engaged citizens within their communities by employing the arts as both a process to understand social issues in the larger community context and a product that contributes to the public dialogue.[30] Through artistic interaction with their environments, students become the investigators and re-creators of their world, making this type of art education exceptionally well suited to support the development of social responsibility and democratic participation.

CBAE has a two-pronged history. One prong of the history was rooted in the established art world and intended for CBAE to provide formal arts training to community members. In rural parts of the United States, such craft schools as Haystack Mountain School of Crafts and Arrowmont School of Arts and Crafts offered CBAE programming. In urban areas, museums and their schools, such as the School of the Art Institute of Chicago, provided classes in the arts for community members. This book, however, draws more heavily from the other historical prong, rooted in the U.S. community-art tradition, which focused on addressing the needs of individuals and communities through art, typically the visual and performing arts.

The Settlement House Movement, which existed in urban areas during the late 1800s, provided basic services and educational opportunities for immigrants. Jane Addams, a famous proponent of the movement, founded the well-known Hull House with Ellen Gates Starr in 1889 in Chicago. In addition to providing extensive social services, language programs, women's and men's groups, a gym, and a library, Hull House also had the first community school of the arts. The National Guild of Community Schools of the Arts, whose mission is "to make high quality arts education available to every interested child and adult in the United States," traces its roots to Hull House.[31] In the early part of the twentieth century, Alfred Arvold, a theater professor at North Dakota State University, also advocated for the arts to be part of ongoing community life. He proposed that community centers act as a unifying force for community members to participate in the arts as well as in science, recreation, and government activities, and he believed that "the fundamental principle back of the community center is the democratization of all art so the common people can appreciate it."[32]

During the Civil Rights Movement, posters, murals, street theater, and puppetry were commonly used for further democratization of the United States. In addition, a number of influential organizations and programs were founded in the 1960s and 1970s that further laid the foundation for CBAE in the United States. For example, the San Francisco Neighborhood Arts Program and the Baltimore Theatre Project[33] were important models. In 1968, Bill Strickland founded Manchester Craftsmen's Guild in Pittsburgh. It is a "multi-discipline, minority-directed, center for arts and learning that employs the visual and performing arts to foster a sense of accomplishment and hope in the urban community."[34] In 1976, Judy Baca, Christina Schlesinger, and Donna Deitch co-founded the Social and Public Art Resource Center (SPARC) in Venice, California—one of the first formal programs to use murals to foster cross-cultural understanding and promote civic dialogue. SPARC "is an arts center that produces, preserves and conducts educational programs about community-based public art works; it espouses public art as an organizing tool for addressing contemporary issues."[35]

Clearly, contemporary CBAE takes many forms. It can be part of a school-based art program that bridges students and their communities, or it can exist in a community setting. There are formalized community-art organizations and informal projects in community settings, ongoing school-based programs, and one-time workshops and events. Regardless of the venue, CBAE settings are places where people come together for "a variety of political, cultural, economic and educational purposes . . . [which] are ultimately directed towards debating and creating the common good."[36] In addition to the aforementioned CBAE organizations that helped set the standard for this work, some noteworthy contemporary community-art organizations, programs, and individuals provide important models. For example, Tim Rollins + K.O.S. (Kids of Survival), a South Bronx–initiated project, uses the arts for both individual transformation and social critique. The group has gained international attention for the content as well as caliber of the work it has created, which can be found in major museum collections worldwide. Just as important as the final product, however, is the process that allows young artists to name and rename their world and use their art as a tool for liberation. New Orleans' Young Aspirations/Young Artists (YA/YA) works with young people and uses art "to empower artistically talented inner-city youth to become professionally self-sufficient through creative expression."[37]

Whether being used to meet educational objectives or to create openings for positive change, community art is a transformative experience that distinctively meets human needs and alters community life. In the following chapters, we present and exemplify strategies extracted from our research on community art, as well as the theory behind the practice. Chapter 2 describes a research-based framework for facilitating community-art projects that, when followed, results in positive outcomes consistent with success indicators for community cultural development.[38] Chapter 3 explores the opportunities and challenges experienced by art practitioners using the framework. Next, chapter 4 provides compelling evidence for the power of community art to impact participants and communities as well as to fulfill meaningful curricular and programmatic goals. In chapter 5, we draw from educational, psychological, and sociological theories to explain the power of the arts to effect change.

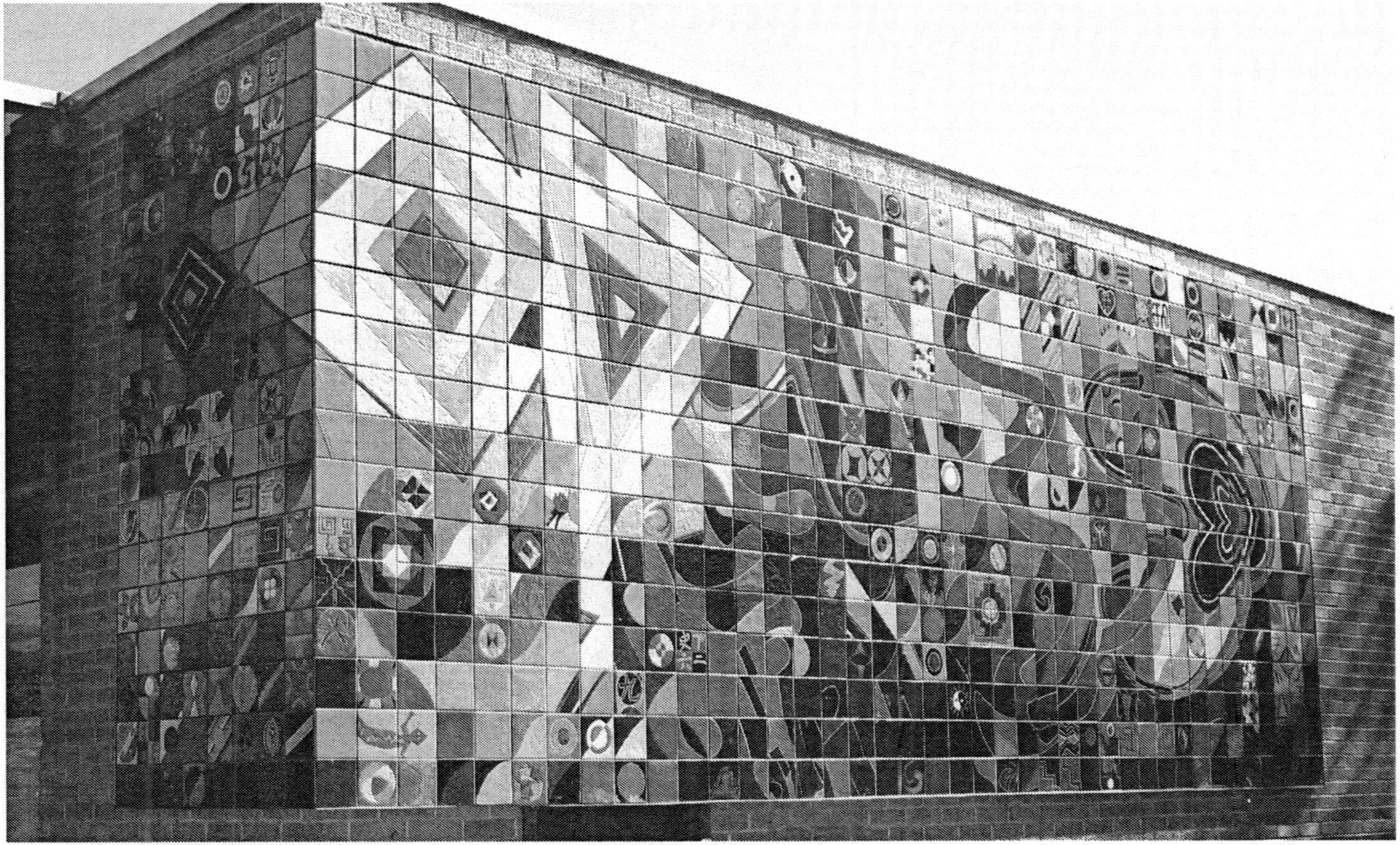

"Youth City Artways" Tile Mural, 2005, Youth City Artways, Salt Lake City Utah, glazed ceramic tile.
Photo credit: Dan Gerhart

Section II offers detailed case studies of artistic media that are particularly compatible with implementing CBAE, including murals, graphics, photography, video, and dance. The case studies found in this book are intended to illustrate the community-art process, highlighting essential steps and offering helpful resources.[39] As you read, we invite you to consider how using community art may enhance the quality of life in your community, organization, or school and bring critically important opportunities for cultural and personal expression to the pursuit of knowledge and understanding in any discipline.

Notes

1. John Dewey, *Art as Experience* (New York: Minton, Balch & Company, 1934), 345–46.
2. National Art Education Association, "Where's the Art?" *National Art Education Association* 2006, www.naea-reston.org/news_advocacy_15flyers.html (accessed September 1, 2006).
3. Judith H. Weitz, *Coming Up Taller: Arts and Humanities Programs for Children and Youth at Risk* (Washington, D.C.: President's Committee on the Arts and Humanities, 1996).
4. Laura Costello, *Part of the Solution: Creative Alternatives for Youth* (Washington, D.C.: National Assembly of State Arts Agencies, 1995).
5. Costello, *Part of the Solution: Creative Alternatives for Youth*, 6.
6. Arlene Goldbard, *New Creative Community: The Art of Cultural Development* (Oakland, Calif.: New Village Press, 2006).
7. June King McFee, "Change and the Cultural Dimensions of Art Education," in *Context, Content, and Community in Art Education: Beyond Postmodernism*, ed. Ronald N. Neperud (New York: Teachers College Press, 1995), 171–92.
8. Erich Fromm, *The Sane Society* (New York: Holt, Rinehart & Winston, 1955), 301–2.
9. Vygotsky, Lev S., *The Psychology of Art* (Cambridge, Mass.: The MIT Press, 1925/1971), 259.
10. Vygotsky, *The Psychology of Art*, 249.
11. Ellen Dissanayake, *Homo Aestheticus* (New York: The Free Press, 1992).
12. Debra Holloway and Beth Krensky, "The Arts, Urban Education, and Social Change," *Education and Urban Society* 33, no. 4 (August 2001): 354–65.
13. Holloway and Krensky, "The Arts, Urban Education, and Social Change," 357.
14. Holloway and Krensky, "The Arts, Urban Education, and Social Change," 358.
15. Fisher, David, "Public Art and Public Space," *Soundings* 79, no. 1–2 (Spring–Summer 1996): 41–57.

16. W. Flood, "Animation: Socio-cultural Community Development in Europe and the United States," (Ph.D. diss., Pennsylvania State University, 1982): 44.

17. Nina Felshin, *But Is It Art? The Spirit of Art as Activism* (Seattle: Bay Press, Inc., 1995).

18. Felshin, *But Is It Art? The Spirit of Art as Activism*, 10.

19. Augusto Boal, *The Rainbow of Desire* (New York: Routledge, 1995), 14.

20. Felshin, *But Is It Art? The Spirit of Art as Activism*.

21. Mev Puleo, "Art as Advocacy," *Breakthrough* (Winter/Summer 1990): 25.

22. Arlene Raven, *Art in the Public Interest* (New York: Da Capo Press, 1993).

23. Eugene Van Erven, *Community Theatre: Global Perspectives* (New York: Routledge, 2001).

24. Malcolm Dickson, *Art With People* (Sunderland, England: AN Publications, 1995); Gay Hawkin, *From Nimbin to Mardi Gras: Constructing Community Arts* (Melbourne, Australia: Allen & Unwin, 1993); Van Erven, *Community Theatre: Global Perspectives*.

25. Tom Duddy, "The Politics of Creativity," *CIRCA* Vol. 68 (Summer 1994): 28–31.

26. Dickson, *Art With People*, 18.

27. Robin Pacific, "This Is Not a Benetton Ad: The Theory of Community Art," *MIX* 23, no. 3 (Winter 1997–1998): 40–43.

28. Robin Pacific, "This Is Not a Benetton Ad: The Theory of Community Art," 40.

29. Theresa Marché, "Looking Outward, Looking in: Community in Art Education," *Art Education* 51, no. 3 (May 1998): 6–13.

30. Kristen Congdon, Doug Blandy, and Paul Bolin, *Histories of Community-Based Art Education* (Reston, Va.: National Art Education Association, 2001).

31. Maryo Ewell, "Some Historical Threads of the Community Arts Story (and Why They Are Important)," July 2001, at www.communityarts.net/readingroom/archivefiles/2002/07/some_historical.php (accessed June 1, 2008).

32. Ewell, "Some Historical Threads of the Community Arts Story (and Why They Are Important)."

33. Arlene Goldbard, "Postscript to the Past: Notes Toward a History of Community Arts," *High Performance* 16, no. 4 (Winter 1993): 23–27.

34. Manchester Craftsmen's Guild organizational mission statement.

35. SPARC organizational mission statement.

36. Congdon, Blandy, and Bolin, *Histories of Community-Based Art Education*, 3.

37. YA/YA organizational mission statement.

38. Goldbard, *New Creative Community: The Art of Cultural Development*, 154.

39. Please note that the case studies documented in section II of the book were not the subjects of the research study presented in section I.

CHAPTER TWO

The Practice of Community Art: From Setting the Stage to Making the Art

Community art is both a process and a product. During the aesthetic experience of community art, a very intentional focus must be placed on the art-making process to ensure an end result that is an authentic cultural production imbued with meaning for the community creating and hosting it. Equal weight must be given to the means and ends of art making to fulfill the change potential that CBAE uniquely offers. In the following pages, we describe the multifaceted role of the art practitioner, explain the steps required to lay the foundation for a successful community-art project, and outline the process for building community and making community art. The information draws from our combined thirty-five years of professional experience in the fields of community art and community development,[1] as well as from three participatory action research projects involving 220 participants, one of which was a rare longitudinal study.[2] The data were collected over a four-year period, during which time we engaged in fieldwork and held fifty-one interviews and twelve focus groups with art practitioners and community-art participants. Our research focused on a mural project, a theater project, and a multimedia park project that the authors co-coordinated with two other art practitioners.[3] The mural project resulted in a permanent installation of sixty circus-themed ceramic tiles at a public library, and the theater project was a play dramatizing Latino culture. The multimedia park project transformed a playground space by installing multiple pieces of artwork such as an entrance, a bench, a garbage can, and a mural designed to be consistent with the theme of peace.

Whether it is a mural or a musical, every community-art project is both *artist led* and *community centered.* Our research shows that community art must be artist led because, while art has transformative capabilities, it alone is not sufficient to cause transformation among individuals working in a community-based setting as a collective. A professional artist or art educator must provide the expert guidance to facilitate the collective, creative process. In the model we are presenting, *community centered* means that the artist or art educator facilitates, rather than directs, participants through a process that encourages them to dream and empowers them to create. Gina,[4] a Latina storyteller in her mid-fifties, describes the balance as "knowing where to use community and where to use the strength of the individual artist." For the remainder of the book, we will use the term *art practitioner* to refer to community artists and art educators.

The Role of the Art Practitioner

The art practitioner is able to be the catalyst for a successful community-art process because he or she uniquely brings the skills, knowledge, and experience required for collaborative art making. Paradoxically, while those drawn to implementing community art believe in the coauthorship of work and the creative potential of all, the power of the art practitioner's role lies in the expert status that he or she holds as an art-world professional who knows how to make and assess art. As a result, participants in community-art projects trust art practitioners to manage the social space and to focus them on community building and art making. Because the art practitioner understands the historical, contextual, and formal elements of art, the community artist has the ability to critique and validate participants' artwork from an informed place. Thus, when the community artist communicates faith in participants' creative abilities and critiques their artwork, group members are more likely to realize their artistic potential because they trust that expert's professional judgment. The community artist's role brings art-world status to a popular setting in a capacity that validates art making by untrained artists through a process that helps participants gain the necessary skills to make high-quality art.

Consistently, art practitioners demonstrate their belief in the power of art and of people's creative potential throughout the artistic process. Ralph, a European-American storyteller in his mid-forties, describes that:

> [participants] may not have had the training and that sort of thing, but they will naturally from their lives have this extraordinary sense of narrative logic . . . and

> seeing that awaken in all folks . . . that is a wonderful kind of thing for everyone in the community to get that they are, that they are naturally artistic.

It is important for art practitioners to speak to participants in a way that illustrates faith in their artistic abilities. The language that art practitioners use during their interactions should reflect the artistic potential the community-art project is intended to foster, thereby affecting how participants see and name themselves. For example, art practitioners typically refer to participants in their artistic roles as dancers, painters, and storytellers, thereby honoring them as having the capacity to be creative peers.

Setting the Stage

Community art is a multifaceted process that includes many levels of social interaction. In a community-based setting, citizens typically are involved in developing and implementing the project with the art practitioner and a local organization that sponsors the planning meetings and hands-on workshops. In a school-based setting, various stakeholders are involved at different stages in the project. Regardless of the setting, organizing CBAE requires extensive planning and coordination, and art practitioners are involved to varying degrees in all aspects of the process. To coordinate CBAE effectively, art practitioners must wear many hats, including those of manager, organizer, recruiter, facilitator, community builder, and, of course, art maker.

Whether community or classroom based, CBAE is a distinct collaborative experience that involves individuals in an authentic participatory process. For the art practitioner, organizing the process begins with *identifying the project goals*. While the goals of making art and building community are inherent, additional project goals typically reflect community needs, school standards, and donor interests. For example, in the multimedia park project, the goals included bringing diverse people together, creating a place for children to play, and teaching youth participants social skills for successful leadership. The project goals articulated by the art practitioner serve as a starting point for cocreating additional goals with participants as the foci of the community-art project.

Another early step of any project is *identifying the community to host or be served* by the art project. An art practitioner may begin with a community in mind based on his or her hometown, school, or workplace, or the priorities of the funding source. If the community or neighborhood is unfamiliar, the art practitioner has the opportunity to map community needs and assets in the target area by reviewing such factors as demographic characteristics, local field-related expertise, and available spaces.[5] The process of mapping community needs and assets also can be a collective classroom or neighborhood activity that builds community and fulfills learning objectives.

Space is an important consideration when determining the host or beneficiary of the community-art project. In a school setting, such venues as the art room, cafeteria, playground, fence, and entries are the strongest options. In the local community, the best display or installation options are public gathering places such as libraries and civic and community centers. Additional viable sites may be found at youth or elder organizations, gardens, or parks. Whatever the options, a setting that ensures the greatest likelihood for success in fulfilling project goals and meeting logistical needs for the artistic medium is critical. For example, in the case of the multimedia park project, we looked for a diverse neighborhood or nonprofit organization that needed a playground, lacked free youth arts programming, and was interested in a year-long collaboration. Ultimately, we chose a mobile home park that had strong support from its manager, a local city councilman, the town library director, and members of the local arts council.

Art practitioners manage the projects by establishing and maintaining relationships with administrators, funders, government officials, nonprofit professionals, and property and business owners. They *inspire gatekeepers and stakeholders* to trust the community-centered process, convince them to be confident about the outcomes, and involve them at appropriate times for input and approval. Support from key stakeholders is critical for success and must be done early in the process. In a school setting, approval from the principal or director, as well as from teachers, parents, custodial staff, and others, is important. In a community, one may seek the endorsement or involvement of city government, a neighborhood board, or community leaders. When working with youth, parents are gatekeepers of any information that is passed on to their children.

Once entrée and stakeholder support are established, art practitioners have varying levels of responsibility for *recruiting participants and sustaining their involvement.* At the neighborhood level, this aspect of organizing involves what storyteller Ralph describes as inspiring "someone about the idea of giving up some personal, private, close-the-door-behind-the-world life. That little bit of precious time you have." Compelling a significant level of involvement requires "something to hook them in and then they can start to get delight in just working side by side with that person and messing up our hands." Our research indicates that people become involved because they are interested in cultural, educational, family, and fun activities. In addition, young people are motivated by their interest in the projects, by their desire to have something to do after school, or by their need to honor parents' or teachers' requests. Motivations are important to consider when designing recruitment methods.

For community art to be effective, there must be a core group of participants, including some type of community leadership, that is committed to participating for the project's duration. The community leader may be the art practitioner working in his or her own school or neighborhood or someone else. Recruiting the core group may be as simple as allocating classroom time for the project or as time intensive as going door to door in a neighborhood and talking with people in their living rooms. Other recruitment approaches include posting information in settings frequented by the target population, such as recreation centers or churches, and advertising in newspapers or neighborhood newsletters. Whether school or community based, effective outreach methods also may include spreading the word through school counselors and administrators, distributing flyers in teachers' mailboxes, making presentations, and holding information tables.

While setting the stage always involves identifying project goals, gaining community entrée, and recruiting participation, organizing a project may also include *securing funding and legal counsel.* Art practitioners may seek funding from parent–teacher associations, schools or school districts, local and state arts councils, local businesses, and art and educational foundations.[6] In cases that require legal counsel and agreements about liability or ownership issues, allowing ample time for the process is important. For example, with the multimedia park project, the sponsoring organization was willing to take legal responsibility for risks associated with the materials and activities involved but wanted to ensure that the owner of the mobile home park would take responsibility for any liability insurance necessary for the completed project. An attorney provided pro bono services to advise on liability issues, draw up contracts, and file documents for us. However, the project was delayed for almost three months while waiting for the owner to sign the necessary agreements. The owner said he was hesitant to continue with the project, and was considering canceling it, because he feared tax increases due to the project's added value. We were able to proceed after numerous phone calls and letters inspired the owner to sign the contracts. As illustrated here, building a planning margin into the timeline is critical for the legal, fiscal, and relational dynamics that are inherent in community-based efforts.

Along with the aforementioned groundwork, setting the stage involves taking preliminary steps to ensure that the community-art projects will be as meaningful as possible. If it is to be "accepted and respected by the community [it must] authentically arise from the experiences of the community."[7] If the art practitioner is a stranger to the community, this requires *conducting research*. The art practitioner must study the population and the setting for the project. Storyteller Gina explains:

> If it's a true collaboration, I think you have to listen to and look at—I mean it's like me when I went into the communities, it's learning about who my partner is visually in terms of geographical space as well as historically, emotionally, psychologically, sociologically, you know—just the kind of demographics there are. You know, what's going on, what are their social issues, what are their political issues right now, what are they struggling with right now. And let them talk to you and you talk to them. [*sic*]

Building Community

The experience of coming together for CBAE, whether in a neighborhood or a classroom, involves a dual emphasis on being creative and building relationships. According to the art practitioners we interviewed, it is important to remind participants throughout the project that "getting to know each other and community building is what this is about." The goal is to create a sense of community around learning about specific topics or solving specific problems through the process of art making. Jerry, a European-American muralist in his forties, likens it to:

> a barn-raising, where people had a real community and if they didn't work together, they wouldn't survive, certainly not flourish. And we're no different. So in that model, people came together to bring their individual skills, whether it was they had a hammer and a nail or they helped cook pies for lunch for the effort, the community came together and built a barn which enhanced the vibrance of the whole community. And yet each person was able to bring their own skills, not get swallowed up in that effort and look at it as something we did and certainly that sense of community is something that manifests itself in a variety of ways beyond the barn; in the case of a community mural, in a variety of ways beyond the artwork. That you simply know your neighbor is something that is so, so important. So actually getting out face to face, meeting your neighbors, working with them, sharing a common experience, ideally a positive experience, where, once again, you worked together to enhance your community. [*sic*]

To lay the foundation for a sense of community, the art practitioner helps participants build awareness about themselves and each other. The first step is to build community by facilitating various *community-building activities and initiatives*, whether the participants have been previously acquainted or not. For example, the multimedia park project began with a "name game" and an exercise in which each participant shared a quality they brought to the group. Next, they defined what community meant to them personally and as a group, and they developed ground rules to help support their conceptions of community as mentioned above. Whenever possible, art practitioners should choose community-building activities that complement the art-making process. Art practitioners can facilitate a positive experience of working with others by engaging in self-definition exercises that help participants learn about and celebrate their own, and the group's, diversity. In the case of the multimedia park project, self-definition exercises consisted of discussions about the different types of diversity existing within the group, such as gender, ethnicity, religion, and family experiences. Exercises highlighted and celebrated the unique attributes of the different participants. Many books and resources provide examples of exercises that may be adapted for community building in a community-art setting.[8]

The art practitioner plays a key role in facilitating connections among diverse others. Brian, a dancer in his mid-twenties, explains that "social interaction between people that wouldn't ordinarily talk is a big part (of my role). Like getting neighbors to talk to each other." When people come together to create art, they build the relationships through talking and telling stories in an environment that allows them to discover their shared humanity and to respect their differences. Caroline, a European-American choreographer in her thirties, believes that regular contact is critical:

> If somebody doesn't show up, call them. And so I say not "Where were you?" but "We missed you." Because I think that doing community building is really delicate and needs a lot of nurturing. And so the idea that somebody is actually part of the community and is missed is a whole different thing from like, "Where were you, you were supposed to be here on Tuesday." And that goes for kids and adults . . . and they're like, "Wow, I mean, you missed me? I'm valuable?" [*sic*]

To create a fully inclusive and responsive community-art project, the art practitioner must act as a facilitator, guiding the process. Art practitioners set the stage by facilitating collectively understood and chosen foci and well-defined norms for social interaction. Knowing how to support groups in successfully thinking and planning to forward their goals is essential.[9] Effective facilitation requires *establishing a clear framework for interaction* within which the community-art project operates. This framework, which must be laid at the project's start, identifies the parameters for community art and sets an empowering context by clarifying the level of participant involvement in decision making. It can be thought of as a bounded social space for engaging in the activities of art making, within which participants have the freedom to make whatever aesthetic and technical choices fall within the purview of that space. To ensure a successful experience, it is important to facilitate participants in *determining their project goals* and *guidelines for interaction*.

Given that a hallmark of community art is empowerment through participation, the art practitioner needs to identify all parameters that might be perceived as limitations during the process and articulate them explicitly at the start of the project. For example, participants may feel disempowered if they engage in a project thinking they have total freedom to create art and only later discover they have only the freedom to choose the theme, not the medium or the placement of the art. Typically, framework boundaries are based on the artist's area of expertise, the resources available for the project, and any other relevant environmental, political, and social variables. The art practitioner's role is to choose parameters appropriate for such factors as age, skill level, cost, time, and installation location. The art practitioner then facilitates the cycle of making inclusive decisions and acting on them in order to create art and build community within that framework throughout the community-art projects.

Strategic questioning is a skill that is extremely helpful for art practitioners to use when facilitating. Strategic questions are questions that make a difference for participants by creating openings for change or movement.[10] Through the use of strategic questioning, art practitioners can guide participants in identifying and planning what they want for themselves and their group or community during the project and can foster participant-generated solutions to challenges that arise among group members during the process of working together. When done properly, facilitation in the community-centered model empowers participants to take ownership of the art. For example, during the multimedia park project, one of the adult volunteers described the following:

> One thing I really learned to focus on was that it was entirely the kids' project. And I think that the volunteers I saw really put the kids' concerns and interests and desires at the forefront and helped without ever saying, "We can't do that" or "That's not allowed" or "I don't think that's a good idea." Every suggestion I felt like was taken seriously and I think the kids realized that people were listening to them and cared about their opinions. [*sic*]

Consequently, the participants were genuinely invested in and committed to the art. Several youth began patrolling the site after all of the artists and volunteers had left to ensure that the area was not vandalized. Also, the participants began seeing themselves as those in charge of the project. For instance, a group of young people was working on an entrance sculpture, and a new neighborhood youth arrived to help out. He asked the artist, "Are you the boss?" Before the art practitioner could reply, a boy who had played a major role in designing the entrance answered, "No, we are."

In addition to having a clear and empowering framework for interaction, a positive community-art experience needs a *safe space* that feels like a nonthreatening and lighthearted social setting. That space must be constructed very deliberately by the words and actions of art practitioners. For example, several art practitioners emphasized the usefulness of providing refreshments. Jerry the muralist explains:

> Food makes people feel safe. It takes the edge off of people's hunger if they're hungry or nervousness if they're nervous and, also when people eat together, a funny little thing occurs. We break bread together and that's kind of a core shared experience that every human being understands without any real intellectualization. [*sic*]

While refreshments represent one commonly used technique for comforting people, art practitioners also must establish nonjudgmental guidelines for interaction. Whether working with adults, young people, or a group of diverse ages, they must establish agreed-upon norms. These interaction guidelines create the foundation for a safe, productive space. They should be created by group members during one of the first project meetings and reflect the behaviors essential for a safe environment. For example, the ground rules created by youth participants and community artists involved in the multimedia park project included:

- Listen
- Everyone participates
- Respect each other
  - Don't talk or laugh while someone else is talking
  - Don't hurt each other
  - No teasing or put-downs
  - No horsing around
  - No fights
  - Don't destroy something that's not yours

- Be quiet when not in the conference room
- Respect library rules
- Be on time; leave on time
- Be prepared

During the mural project, Andrew, a sixteen-year-old Navajo participant, described that his experience felt different from the critical dynamics of other group experiences because group members were encouraged to share ideas and to "show things [to each other] so we didn't feel stupid." Fernanda, a fifteen-year-old Latina dancer from the theater project, says that she learned "not to judge, [but] to help out and make someone feel better."

In addition to providing a safe space for exploration, discovery, and creative self-expression, art practitioners need to be intentional about creating an open, playful environment. Group members should be encouraged to communicate openly about their ideas and to share their work. At the onset, the art practitioners set the stage for cooperative and enriching group experiences. Statements by art practitioners like "If it is fun, creativity naturally will evolve" and "With art, if we share, we learn" lay the foundation for the interactions among group members to be playful and relaxed from the beginning. Jerry explains the importance of fun from his perspective as an art practitioner of twenty-five years:

> Fun in my estimation is the most underrated word in the English language. To have fun, you have to relax, you have to open up, you have to take a risk, you have to expose yourself and who you really are, so those are all very deep, involved things and yet if you're successful, it's so light that, I think it's just the greatest way for people to really get to know each other. Art is wonderful that way. Art can start out as a chore and if you surveyed people, well you're going to do a permanent public piece of art, a lot of them right away, they'll freak out. So you have to be careful not to approach it that way. We're just gonna have fun and we're gonna do these things and teach 'em some skills and make sure to try to incorporate fun as the learning tool. So I think people learn about that. They learn that they're not as limited as we all tend to think of ourselves. "Yeah, I could be a permanent public artist, how about that?" . . . If an experience can be designed or if you're fortunate enough to have an experience with your neighbors in community work be fun, then it really is very positive, your memories of it are positive and the [art] as a symbol becomes very positive. [*sic*]

Ultimately, an atmosphere that is safe and fun allows participants to explore relationships and to express themselves creatively when coming together in the free space of art.

In addition to an explicit focus on building community through the essential elements outlined above, the art practitioner facilitates participatory decisions throughout the community-art process that naturally foster connections for participants. *Participatory decision making* is a fundamental practice in helping people feel valued during community building and art making.[11] A participatory decision-making process allows each participant to contribute his or her ideas in a way that fosters understanding among diverse perspectives and interests. While this may require more time to facilitate, the inclusive process compels a sense of shared responsibility and ownership that contributes to the success of the community-art projects. Participatory decision making also can increase efficiency and productivity at later stages in the community-art project because of the participants' investment and alignment in the process.

A range of participatory input can be employed in the decision-making process. For example, in the consultative approach, the art practitioner solicits input from participants and then makes the decision. A second technique allows the group to choose within structured options. A third option allows the group total freedom to choose with the structured support of a facilitated decision-making process. Regardless of the level of participatory involvement, the participants' input must be heard, valued, and responded to. Most art practitioners in our study used consensus to empower participants to feel ownership and to be invested in the work. Jerry the muralist observes, "Consensus is difficult, but better than democracy because democracy creates a minority which can become disenfranchised."

During decision making, art practitioners must balance focus and flexibility by returning the group to realistic options and responding to their suggestions. For example, an art practitioner may employ participatory decision making with the participants to choose the content and medium for their community-art project within a range of viable options. The mural project was predetermined to be a mural for a library wall, and neighborhood residents freely chose to use a circus theme with ceramic tiles. In the theater project, neighborhood residents knew their play needed to be an intergenerational expression of culture and chose to use poetry, drama, music, and dance. Adrienne, a twenty-seven-year-old Italian-American painter, describes an example of a consensus outcome determined through a participatory process:

> In working with youth from a low-income community, the youth decided on . . . a creative and great way to do a collaborative ceramic tile piece. In their design, the kids didn't all have to agree on one huge image. They decided on the central

> image, theme and message, which was "Peace is Possible," and they decided that different kids would get to decide on their own personal images of what peace meant to them. And then those were painted on individual tiles surrounding the central image. [*sic*]

By using such techniques as consensus, facilitation, and strategic questioning, art practitioners can effectively involve participants in co-creating community art. An authentic participatory process results in relationships and art that are meaningful, relevant, and vibrantly alive as the full self-expression of individuals coming together as a community.

Making Art

While the previous sections focused on how to set the stage for successful community-art projects and how to facilitate the community-building process, the following section focuses on how to provide an authentic art-making experience that balances skill building and role taking with the process of making professional-quality art. As mentioned earlier, this type of experience or programming, which enables participants to develop new skills, to envision new possibilities, and to fulfill the intrinsic human need to create, yields tremendous results for individuals and their communities. However, these results are a function of the unique role that the art practitioner plays in bringing the skills, knowledge, and expertise required to collaborate successfully with others in art making. For CBAE to be as fulfilling and powerful an experience as possible, the art-making process must (1) be intentionally situated, (2) combine high expectations with comprehensive artistic training, and (3) result in interaction between viewers and the works of art.

Situating Community Art

Situating community art involves determining the audience for the artwork, envisioning its thematic content and form, and conducting relevant research. As mentioned earlier, before beginning this phase of CBAE, of critical importance is that the art practitioner has established a framework for interaction. Within this bounded space is where group members make thematic, aesthetic, and technical choices through a participatory decision-making process that is informed by the artist's area of expertise, the resources available for the project, and any other relevant environmental, political, or social variables.

Community-art projects most often begin as possibilities outlined by art practitioners. The authentic community experience is then co-created along a continuum of different levels of community involvement. Participant choice ranges from total freedom to determine all elements of the community-art project to focused freedom within predetermined options. As art practitioners, we are challenged to balance personal style with community involvement in the interplay between CBAE's being artist led and community centered during these steps in the process. Jerry the muralist explains:

> For example, my tendency would be to limit the palette of any mural as a way to unify it. But that's something that the group will come to and they'll have that commitment of having come to it themselves through experimentation, exploration, and knowledge. You've got to be ready to back off what your personal agenda is. But you need the framework or else it's too wide.

A critical early step of situating the art is to *determine the audience* to be served by the art. The audience may be determined by the funder or another stakeholder in advance, or it may be chosen freely by the participants. Of course, the audience always includes the participants. Whatever the case, taking the time to identify and use the audience to inform choices throughout the project is very important. For example, during the multimedia park project, participants surveyed community residents about their art interests before choosing their activities. In the theater project, because family and friends were the primary audience, the costumes of traditional women's wraps (los huipiles) were designed with embroidered memories from the lives of the women wearing them. Always in CBAE, effective art practitioners encourage participants to make the art mean something to them personally.

The next component essential to situating the art involves *envisioning the content and form.* As mentioned earlier, while art in and of itself has transformative capabilities, it alone is not sufficient to provoke transformation in a community-art setting. The professional artist or art practitioner catalyzes the artistic process by authorizing and inspiring participants to envision and to dream. Brian the dancer describes it in the following way:

> Art is the search for beauty. And I think people look for that and I think that's part of what I offer is, that you know, you too can open this. Dreaming is OK. Sometimes I get kind of poetic, it's hard to really put the right words to it. But I think letting people know that dreams are valid things and that you actually can do something with it [is important]. [*sic*]

To envision powerfully involves brainstorming ideas and exposing group members to different images in order to expand their conceptions of what is possible thematically, technically, and aesthetically. Envisioning can occur through discussion-based brainstorming sessions and arts-based exercises such as drawing, creating collages, photography, and computer-generated graphics.

In the mural project, participants determined the theme as the art practitioner facilitated them in brainstorming a variety of possibilities and exploring each option's implications in the context of the project goals. The participants then chose to focus on neighborhood history as a way to unite diverse backgrounds and to foster pride among themselves and others in the target audience. During the multimedia park project, on the other hand, there was a predetermined issue of peace. In this case, the participants explored different meanings of peace, such as interpersonal peace through conflict resolution and community peace through community organizing. After exploring all of the different types of peace, the group selected inner peace and interpersonal peace as the foci of the project. Adrienne the painter describes designing the vision with youth participants:

> We talked about whether or not peace was possible, period, and the kids were thinking, "No, not in the world, and not in the United States." They thought that it *might* be possible in [our state] and agreed that peace was definitely possible in their [mobile home park]. That turned out to be the theme then for their piece of art that they wanted to create.

Understanding what was possible was the first step for students in working toward creating new visions. The youth used art as a tool for expressing their views of and hopes for peace when words failed them. Several exercises helped the young people explore, discuss, and create drawings about different types of peace. Most often the young people expressed their ideas in visual, rather than verbal, ways. They drew pictures of their community and included some of the issues facing its residents. These images were used as tools for students to talk about their community and to create the foundation for envisioning possibilities for positive change. Consequently, they decided to design a space where individuals could feel peaceful and where peaceful interactions among people would be more likely to occur.

Once the content or theme is chosen, the process for determining artistic form includes selecting the medium and the installation treatment or performance venue. For example, in the theater project, the art practitioners presented the proposal of a play as a cultural representation that could include dance and narration, among other ideas that participants generated and subsequently chose from. As Aida, a Latina visual artist in her mid-forties, shares, "The community members wanted special, important things to the heart—for example, pottery, weaving, Nahuatl song." Given their expertise, Aida and her colleague Consuela then explored how best to match neighborhood residents' interests with project resources to shape the community-art project. They took into account such factors as the actual number of people wanting to participate and the amount of time available to learn and rehearse. During the design of the artwork for the multimedia park project, one of the issues for the participants to consider was how the pieces might invite interaction between park visitors and the artwork. Some pieces, such as the bench, were clearly interactive, but other works took much discussion and many sketches to arrive at results facilitating interaction. In the case of the tile mural, the participants chose many individual tiles that would inspire people to spend time looking, and for the entrance sculpture they listed the names of all the participants who helped create it so that people would stop and read.

Last, whether the participants in CBAE are students or neighborhood residents, there is always some *research to conduct* in order to most effectively and responsibly produce high-quality, meaningful art. The research phase is particularly important for classrooms, where the project is done in the context of a standards-based inquiry with subject-specific topics informing the thematic content, and discipline-specific media informing the process. The research may be on the community, an issue relevant to the theme, or the artistic method to be used to express what participants have envisioned for themselves and their community. For example, with the multimedia park project, participants studied the history of peace parks, researched representations of images, and learned about and practiced relevant design technology. The multimedia park project met standards for language arts (with a focus on oral communication, reading, and writing), social studies (with a focus on citizenship and social change), and science (with a focus on water cycles and native plants). The integrated unit was taught using a service-learning model that allowed students to deepen their understanding of academic objectives while engaging in the community service of addressing the needs of a low-income neighborhood. Through hands-on activities, the participants developed critical-thinking, conflict-resolution, community-organizing, leadership, and artistic skills to support their designing, planning, and building of the multimedia park.

Combining High Expectations with Comprehensive Artistic Training

Once participants determine a shared vision of content and form, the art practitioner supports participants in technically and logistically expressing their vision artistically. Developing their vision and the creative capacity to express that vision involves mentorship, apprenticeship, and professional development. For the process to proceed successfully, art practitioners must have high performance expectations, expose participants to appropriate artistic training, and provide guided practice to help participants progress from novices to capable artists. Training takes place during the art-making process in many different ways, including interaction with professional artists, use of professional art materials, study of art history relevant to the project, mastery of the artistic medium, and critique. The skills-building component of the artistic process typically scaffolds, beginning simply and building to more complex, creative activities. Brian the dancer explains it as starting with the "beginner's mind." For example, during the mural project, the art practitioner began with markers or crayons while brainstorming and then moved the neighborhood residents to explore different media such as ceramics and mosaics.

In the multimedia park project, part of the training for the artwork design involved viewing slides of peace-related and youth-created works of art, reading art history books, and learning about artistic movements dealing with social change. Four professional artists supported the youth participants in creating five pieces of public art: a tile mural, a mosaic and handmade tile walkway, a garbage can, a bench, and an entrance sculpture. The art practitioners played a dual role. First, they were able to teach the youth about techniques, materials, art history, and artistic critique in which the youth engaged as they were collaboratively designing the works of art. Second, the art practitioners gave the young people a glimpse into the professional life of an artist and a connection with the art world. The artists initially showed slides about how different art forms had been used to convey messages and how their medium of expertise could be used in public spaces. After the artists shared slides and described the artistic process they would be facilitating, participants chose different art committees with which to work.

Once participants show a serious interest in learning about and engaging in the artistic process, art practitioners can and should treat them as colleagues, which tends to catapult the level to which participants envision themselves as having something of value to contribute. As mentioned earlier, community art involves relating to participants as and calling them *artists*, a term that cannot be used lightly. The art practitioner then has the responsibility to train them rigorously and to expect that their involvement befit the title. In addition to relating to participants as artist colleagues and cultivating artistic proficiency, an aspect of artistic rigor involves providing access to authentic materials. In each of the case studies, the art practitioners ensured that participants used professional materials from the design phase through the creation of the pieces. The art practitioners were explicit about the types of materials being used and the fact that professional artists used the same materials. One of the architects who worked with the participants hosted a field trip to his office, where he talked about architecture and design, let the youth experiment with design software, and gave each youth a "designer's pen." The young people were able to envision themselves as designers and, as such, a few of the older boys asked very detailed questions about model building. In another project, youth were entrusted with expensive, delicate photography and artistic equipment; when such high expectations were held for them, they most often behaved in ways befitting the artist role. One mother comments about her understanding of the process:

> At the beginning, I didn't understand all of the time involved in doing the artwork. It wasn't a rush, let's get this done so it looks good kind of thing, it was more of a slow down and enjoy the process of doing the artwork because that's where the learning is taking place. [*sic*]

As participants, both young and old, evolve their skills with creative self-expression and become more confident with the discipline standards for art making, they shift from seeing themselves as novices to seeing themselves as a capable artists.

Completing the Community-Art Project

Completing any community-art project involves a *formal unveiling* that results in interaction between viewers and the work of art. As stated earlier, Dewey suggests that experience goes beyond the creative phase of art making and occurs each time the finished artistic product is viewed.[12] He asserts that a triadic relationship exists between the work of art, the viewer, and the creator, and that "the work of art is complete only as it works in the experience of others [rather] than the one who created it."[13] CBAE cannot be considered complete until there has been some change in the physical landscape or transformation of the physical space through a production that is witnessed. For the purposes of our writing, we will call this witnessing the *unveiling*.

An unveiling serves as public affirmation of what group members have built and created together. The unveiling typically involves the art practitioner, key supporters and stakeholders, relevant public figures, and participants and community members. It is the art practitioner who plays the key role of ensuring that information about the project gets to the general public and that there is a proper unveiling that gets the artistic product to its intended audience. An unveiling fulfills the transformative power of art by engaging an audience and eliciting their responses in interaction with the art as viewers. While the art-making process helps participants envision themselves as artists by supporting the creation of professional-quality artwork, the unveiling reinforces those newly formed perceptions by allowing participants to witness others viewing their artwork and them as artists. An unveiling is critical to solidifying the shift from novice to artist. This is also the time in the process to acknowledge individuals and organizations that contributed to the project's success.

From the research sites used for this book, the theater project was performed several times, including two performances for 750 elementary school children and one performance for people from the neighborhood. There was a dedication ceremony at the local public library for the mural project that approximately fifty men, women, and children attended. The finished art pieces of the multimedia park project changed the physical landscape of the community park and publicly portrayed the multiple visions and messages of peace that the participants created. Its unveiling involved a community presentation by the participants about their experience, accompanied by a tour of the park. Seventy people attended, including the sponsoring city councilman and the local press.

The creation of a work of community art is truly an accomplishment to be celebrated. *Celebration* provides participants with the opportunity to appreciate each other and to be honored in an audience environment for their commitment and creativity. Whether coupled with the unveiling or scheduled separately, such events usually include music, food, and an introduction or presentation by members of the community-art project and other key community figures. During a celebration, it is important that all of the participants are acknowledged or recognized for their contributions in some way. It also is critically important that there be *reflection and evaluation* of the experience by the participants to provide a sense of completion and to inform the quality of future endeavors.

As mentioned earlier, community art is both a process and a product. Following the research-based framework for facilitating successful CBAE outlined in this chapter yields tremendous results for individuals and communities, which are discussed in the following chapter. Table 2.1 summarizes the phases of the process with their elements for art practitioners.

Table 2.1. Framework for Successful Community-Art Projects

Phase	*Elements*
Setting the Stage	• Identifying the project goals • Securing the community to host or be served • Gaining entrée with gatekeepers and stakeholders • Recruiting participants *Throughout:* • *Conducting community research* *As needed:* • *Securing funding or legal counsel*
Building Community	• Facilitating community-building activities and initiatives • Establishing a clear framework for the project • Determining additional project goals • Determining clear guidelines for interaction • Ensuring a safe and lighthearted environment *Throughout:* • *Facilitating participatory decision making*
Making Art	• Situating the art ☐ Determining the audience ☐ Envisioning the content and form ☐ Conducting content and form research • Setting high expectations • Providing comprehensive artistic training • Completing the project ☐ Hosting a formal unveiling ☐ Having a celebration ☐ Reflecting and evaluating

Notes

1. The community-centered process outlined in this book draws from the INVST Community Leadership Program curriculum that was developed by Seana Lowe Steffen between 1994 and 2006, when she was founding director of INVST Community Studies at the University of Colorado, Boulder. The Project YES curriculum cited in this book was created by Beth Krensky and Carole MacNeil between 1990 and 2000, when they were the organization's co-founders and co-directors.

2. Beth Krensky, "An Act of Hope: Developing Social Responsibility through Issue-Oriented Community-Based Art Education" (Ph.D. diss., University of Colorado, Boulder, 2002); Seana Lowe, "The Art of Community Development" (Ph.D. diss., University of Colorado at Boulder, 2002).

3. In addition to this book's two authors, the multimedia park project was coordinated with Juliet Biagi and Carole MacNeil. This eighteen-month-long project was organized with Project YES and involved professional artists, a local middle school,

the public library, an architectural firm, civic organizations, graduate education students, and volunteers.

4. All names used are pseudonyms.

5. John P. Kretzmann and John L. McKnight, *Building Communities from the Inside Out: A Path Toward Finding and Mobilizing a Community's Assets* (Evanston, Ill.: Institute for Policy Research, 1993).

6. Please see *Appendix F, General Resources*, for more information about funding.

7. Olivia Gude, "Beyond Monological Monuments: The Possibility of Heteroglossia in Public Space," *Public Art Review*, no. 12 (Spring/Summer 1995): 40.

8. See Karl Rohnke's book that combines many of his previously published initiatives: Karl Rohnke, *Funn 'n Games* (Dubuque, Iowa: Kendall/Hunt Publishing Co., 2004).

9. Sam Kaner, *Facilitator's Guide to Participatory Decision-Making* (Gabriola Island, B.C., and Philadelphia: New Society Publishers, 1996).

10. See Fran Peavey's chapter on strategic questioning: Tova Greene, Peter Woodrow, and Fran Peavey, *Insight and Action: How to Discover and Support a Life of Integrity and Commitment to Change* (Gabriola Island, B.C.: New Society Publishers, 1994).

11. For additional information on how to facilitate participatory decisions, see Kaner's *Facilitator's Guide to Participatory Decision-Making.*

12. John Dewey, *Art as Experience* (New York: Minton, Balch & Company, 1934).

13. Dewey, *Art as Experience*, 106.

CHAPTER THREE

The Art Practitioner: Making the Most of Opportunities and Challenges

By facilitating a meaningful process and ensuring a high-quality outcome, the art practitioner plays a leadership role that is critical to the success of community-art projects. As mentioned in chapter 1, art making by artists working together with people who do not define themselves as artists is an activity that challenges the boundaries of the status hierarchy in the traditional art world. Consequently, artists who choose to be community artists are what sociologist Howard S. Becker calls "mavericks," or professionals who are members of the traditional art world by training but choose to pursue endeavors the art world does not normatively integrate or support.[1]

The role of community artist as a marginalized member of the traditional art world is a complex one. However, the community artist's experience is rewarding enough to inspire lifelong careers in the field. In this chapter, we discuss the nature of the art practitioner's experience with community art. Specifically, we elucidate the complexities art practitioners face in negotiating boundaries, the factors that positively benefit them, and the challenges they encounter. We end with several recommendations for overcoming difficulties on the job.

Blurred Boundaries

While community art is experiential and inclusive by design, it is foremost and fundamentally an artistic endeavor that demands technical expertise, creative vision, and professional experience to fulfill its purpose. The effectiveness of community art rests on the professionalism of the art practitioner as an artist first and as a community builder second. As a result, art practitioners experience dilemmas in navigating the boundaries between the dual focus of community building and art making. Caroline explains the difficulty she often faced as a choreographer:

> And the honest truth is that if you don't do the rehearsal part the piece doesn't get made, and I think the piece does have a lot of benefit for the community members . . . but there's only so much time. But it is challenging to figure out how, you know, building community and making art on a deadline are not necessarily interacting goals. And so to make them interacting goals is challenging. But I think it is possible to do and I think we've done it successfully. But I think that sometimes you do lose a little of one or the other back and forth. [*sic*]

Several community artists in this study distinguish between "art participators" and "art makers" in describing the frustrations they faced doing both community building and art making. For some, knowing that participants in community-art projects were not being allowed the opportunity to study art as a tradition or to learn art as a discipline left them doubting that the participants achieved the aesthetic standards of real art makers. They wanted to teach technical skills and train participants to be authentic art makers but were unable to do so because of scarcities of time and money. In this case, the ideological boundaries of community art become blurred between the belief in universal creative capacity and the practice of disciplined artistic development. Community artists also wrestle with their own standards for growth and development. Sometimes repetition of the same types of projects becomes boring and mundane. As a result, art practitioners may seek new ways to make the work artistically interesting.

Unquestionably, the most important aspect of the art practitioner's role as artist is to provide the artistic or creative vision for the community-art project. In working to accomplish a truly inclusive process that is artist driven, the boundaries of aesthetic standards are confronted regularly. While there is much to appreciate and learn from nonartists as they express their creativity, there is also much to teach them in pursuit of art as a technical product. For Gina the storyteller, as the one in charge of the artistic vision and the aesthetic quality, negotiating the boundaries between popular art and professional art was the hardest part of her job:

> And you push it a little further, just push it a little further. And you have to keep doing that until you [have a strong piece]. I mean whatever it is, even

> though you are collaborating with a community, you should be proud of what you're doing. By the same token, community work really done by the people in a way gets watered down because the artist somehow gets held back because they want the people to create the piece. So you get meaningful pieces but you don't necessarily get the discussion or the dialogue that the vision pushed. [*sic*]

As mavericks, community artists consistently are choosing and crossing boundaries in professional life. Typically, art practitioners are drawn to the practice of community art by a commitment to make a positive difference. At the most basic level, their impact is from inspiring others to express themselves creatively. At the most profound level, art practitioners are challenging societal power relations and inspiring others to take action for positive change. However, as professional artists whose training and status to validate the community-art process are given by the dominant structure of the traditional art world, the benefits and challenges are highly interconnected. For example, while a benefit from community art is the transformative impact of participants' seeing themselves as artists, the corresponding challenge is that those who have been trained in the high-art world may experience dissonance in hearing untrained people give themselves the prestigious title of "artist." A professionally trained artist is an expert who has studied and worked to earn the respected title of professional artist, yet art practitioners typically want everyone to see themselves as artistic and creative beings, which inadvertently tears down the wall between the high-art world and the community-art world.

In addition, since an artist's reputation is based on the aesthetic value of previous works of art,[2] it is not uncommon for art practitioners to wrestle with the realities of diluting the value of their names by having multiple names attached to a piece of art. While those faced with the internal struggle recognize the liabilities that co-creativity means for career success, community artists generously share the stage because of an appreciation for the positive impact that collective ownership has on each person claiming the artwork.

Creative Fulfillment

Choosing to share in the experience of community art enhances the lives of art practitioners in several ways, both personally and professionally. Foremost among the rewards is the opportunity to make a positive difference. Given that community art serves as a vehicle for individual and collective social change, art practitioners can fulfill their needs or desires to serve others in creative and meaningful ways. For example, Gina the storyteller explains:

> It's just this amazing need I have to make a difference in the community. I just grew up with that, you know. I thought about curing cancer and when I realized that I couldn't do that, then I decided I'd do community art. I have this need that I have a role in my community to, you know, do something. To help. [*sic*]

Most community artists express great satisfaction in helping others by sharing their expertise and talents. By doing so, art practitioners witness participants' shift in their view of themselves as artists and appreciation of art at new levels. Sue, a European-American stained-glass artist in her late forties, states:

> One reason that I wanted to do it was I wanted to turn other people on to what happens when you do art and the joy that comes from doing it. I mean I already see that happening in some ways, you know, people taking pride in what they've done. [*sic*]

In addition, art practitioners are rewarded by the opportunity for community involvement with others. Tremendous benefit results from meeting people, learning about the lives of those who are new or unfamiliar, and being part of the process of building community with them. Weaving a web of community through coming together and creating art is a great gift. Involvement with others also counters the isolation that professional artists typically face. Working with others results in community artists' feeling integrated into their communities and satisfying what muralist Jerry describes as a "fundamental human need for connection."

Many community artists observe that community art also benefits their careers in several important ways. While community art seldom results in significant financial gains, it often provides material benefits, such as artistic supplies and permanent works of publicly displayed art. In addition, community art can be a rich source of new ideas that foster expanded creative expression. Community artists derive inspiration from seeing and doing things in different ways through the collective creative process. One community artist likened the opportunity to be surrounded by the rich creativity of collaborative art making to Picasso's method of opening up his studio to young artists. Brian the dancer spoke about how his creativity was enhanced by "just seeing how nontrained artists make decisions, creative decisions. That just blows my mind every time. The decisions a nontrained artist makes are very different from a trained person, and I love seeing that over and over again. That challenges the way that I make decisions, so that's something that I just enjoy."

In addition, the experience of doing community art enhances community artists' effectiveness with their media and expands the repertoire of their skills. For example, a stained-glass artist might venture into mosaics for a community-art project and thereby gain the technical experience of the new medium through the process, or a storyteller might discover techniques from working with community members that make his or her own creative efforts flow more easily. Caroline appreciates benefits for both herself and her company as a dancer and choreographer:

> I've been really inspired artistically. I think my work has evolved a lot in a good way because of my involvement in community art. And especially also, I mean I've done a lot of work as an artist in schools just watching how untrained people make dances, and the beauty in what they make, whether they're kids or adults or mixed groups, is really, really beautiful. . . . But I think that for a long time I felt like my professional work had to be really separate or something. And now I actually have taken dancers into my company that I have met in community projects and I've had sort of adjunct dancers perform in my, you know, I have like a core company of technically trained, professional dancers who can do anything I ask them to do technically. But then I have an adjunct group of dancers who are people who aren't professionally trained but are great performers that I actually put in my professional work and most of those people I met in the community dance projects. . . . But what I think is interesting is that artistically I've moved to really liking the look of having nontrained people next to the trained people in my work. And I feel like they add an energy that's really wonderful, too. So I think for me as an artist it's enabled me to sort of grow and be a little more flexible with my art and look at new opportunities. [*sic*]

For many art practitioners, having the art placed in the public domain may be a new experience of transforming the physical landscape of an area and of having completed work showcased in a community setting. It may also be an opportunity to develop shared vision with community members in a way that fosters a helpful investment in the arts. Beyond those who are full participants, community buy in can come from those who assist in related activities ranging from offering advice to spearheading a drive for materials. For school-based arts projects, this type of community interaction tends to cultivate support for the larger school art program.

For art practitioners in the classroom, CBAE yields the unique benefit of being able to learn about, become engaged in, and contribute to the community.

It provides the arts practitioner with opportunities to make education relevant and meaningful to students, because the community-art project can address or serve a true community need. For example, the multimedia park project began as a collaboration between a community-based arts organization and a middle school. One teacher remarked that the unit allowed her to increase her own understanding of the community in which she taught as well as provided her with the opportunity to teach in a way that was consistent with her commitment to use education as a tool for civic engagement.[3]

Common Challenges

To experience the positive difference community art uniquely makes for all involved, artist and participant alike, art practitioners must overcome and transform various challenges. The most common challenges involve inspiring and sustaining participation, balancing the role's responsibilities, bridging differences among diverse participants, and bearing responsibility for the success of the project.

Inspiring Participation

The obstacles to openness to community-art involvement can seem overwhelming to those seeking to inspire active engagement. Not surprisingly, the most frequent barrier to would-be participants in community-based settings is scarcity of time. The focus group exchange below illustrates what art practitioners face in that area:

> Ralph the storyteller: There is not much of a notion of leisure time, and the idea of being in community art is something that belongs in leisure time.
>
> Gina the storyteller: Because of this perception of art as a luxury and especially within neighborhoods that are low-economic neighborhoods, there is the culture of poverty there that it's hard to allow for that luxury of art. And what I have enjoyed is then targeting the age group that is not the child because the assumption within the neighborhoods is that it's for the kids and you know, "How wonderful, but we don't have time because we are working two jobs and we don't have and we don't have and we don't have." It's the whole system of lack and scarcity. [*sic*]

In addition to "lack and scarcity," art practitioners frequently are faced with overcoming beliefs rooted in socioeconomic status differences that define art as unavailable or inappropriate. People often perceive that doing art is risky because of their notions of what it takes to be creative and who can succeed at doing art.

Typically, those most interested in participating in community art at the onset are either young or well educated or both. Indeed, the most powerful demographic predictors of artistic interest and participation in local artistic activities are gender and education, with women[4] and college-educated people demonstrating significantly higher involvement.[5] Therefore, the challenge may be to involve community-art participants who fit the demographic profiles that the stakeholders have identified.

During the process of developing a community-art project, art practitioners also may experience difficulty in discerning who the formal and informal leaders are for their setting and in securing committed participation to organize and implement the project by those stakeholders. It is important that any collaborating leadership, whether formally affiliated with a school or neighborhood organization or informally authorized to influence others, is someone who is genuinely interested in the project and who is a respected, trusted, integral part of the organization or neighborhood.

For example, early in the process of coordinating the multimedia park project, we distributed 135 surveys, but only one household completed and returned it. Later, during the months when the project was fully under way, we learned that some parents did not trust the manager of the mobile home park and that others thought that the manager was not around enough. One parent complained about the management's involvement as "a source of frustration and negativity and disappointment . . . it really brought me down and it seemed like a constant obstacle to overcome." Since the residents thought we were closely connected with the management as our entrée, they naturally did not want to be involved initially.

In addition, because residents doubted that anything positive would happen in their community, they were hesitant to believe in the community-art project. It was only when youth and adults saw the physical changes occurring that they believed it could actually happen and that they could be active participants. After the community-art project was completed, one mother said that there had been a sense of hopelessness in the mobile home community, and that the community-art experience had left her with "more hope. The hope that there are good things in this world and that there could be better things." She felt the project was "a catalyst to push people off the couch to do something." Many of the residents confided that they had never met anyone in their community and had never gotten involved there until the community-art project.

Sustaining Participation

Once a core group is set to participate, sustaining participation can be difficult, particularly in nonclassroom settings. If the participation is discontinuous, the art practitioner must become the common link in the transition from one group to the next. Discontinuity can occur because participants do not understand that being part of a community-art project necessitates taking an active role. Other times, parents may not understand that their children's involvement is a commitment and that people are counting on their child as part of the group. In some cases, discontinuity occurs because art practitioners do not meet the diverse needs and interests of the participants during the process. Laura, a European-American photographer in her mid-forties, explains the balance:

> I think that also it has to be this weird line between it being nonthreatening and also challenging. It can't be boring or juvenile. It has got to be personal enough that it appeals to every person there and that every person can search themselves, from a six-year-old to an eighty-year-old, and find something meaningful to add into the art-making process, whether that's a story that they are telling or a movement that they are contributing, but it has to be significant. It can't be sort of done on a level where it turns somebody off or it feels either too challenging, like by being too threatening, like they have to divulge the most personal thing that they think of. . . . So I think that is a challenging community exercise [in] finding that level of personal and artistic challenge. [*sic*]

Whether set in a classroom or in the community, community art requires collaboration. Consequently, varied expectations for participation originate from collaborators such as funders, sponsoring organizations, or schools and the participants or community artists themselves. Often, the source of financial support for a project specifies involvement with a diversity of ages, ethnicities, and incomes or with underserved segments of society, such as gang members or households in poverty. One of the most common challenges to the community artist's experience is to inspire participation among those residents who meet the demographic criteria identified by a funder as the target audience. Most art practitioners also want diverse participation, as the following focus group interaction illustrates:

> Caroline the choreographer: I find that sometimes the people who come are the people who are already really involved in dance in one way or another or have done it in some way or, you know, it's been their lifelong love. Even if

they have never taken a formal class, they have done it, and I really want to reach those people who aren't like that, but those people want to play soccer. They have no interest in dance.

Laura the photographer: Well, I guess I want to reach everybody, not just people who I might label as on the margin or not having access to art, and I want to mix them all up together, because even people who have had extensive training in the arts. I mean they maybe had a restricted classical training and were told that they were not good enough to make it, quote unquote, and maybe they have a natural way of expressing themselves that's like a classical type of training model but just really didn't access it, so I want everybody. I want people who think they are pros. I want people who never held a camera. I want people who have trouble paying rent. I want rich people, middle-class people. I want them all in there together 'cause I want them to develop as individuals, but I also want to bust stereotypes and the way that that happens for me is when we all get together in a room together and wrangle with what's our subject matter and what are we doing and how are we going to present it. [*sic*]

There is also a challenge of matching the art practitioner's profile with the funder's or sponsor's expectations for expertise. For example, the funder may specify that the art practitioner needs to be a found-objects sculptor or an established public artist as well as a member of the neighborhood.

Balancing the Responsibilities of the Role

To facilitate community-art projects, art practitioners must successfully negotiate responsibilities with many different people. As mentioned in chapter 2, art practitioners often play the roles of recruiter and organizer. In addition, art practitioners act as the managers of the projects by working with funders, administrators, government officials, property owners, business owners, and nonprofit professionals. Art practitioners encourage the "powers that be" to trust the process, convince them to be confident in the impending outcomes, and involve them at appropriate times for input or approval. Sometimes the various stakeholders exert what may feel like competing or unreasonable demands on the art practitioner. Gina the storyteller expresses her frustration in a focus group:

How do I know that this arts project changed behavior or did it just keep a kid out of trouble from 3:30 to 4:30 because it was an after-school program? Is that worth it? If it kept them out of trouble, I'm going to say yeah, it was worth it. Was it long term? I have no idea. I mean, we don't have enough money to buy paints and tissue paper that we're not borrowing and stealing, let alone to do

> surveys. But I understand we're being funded from the private sector or the public sector, they want to know, they, meaning the funders, want to know, "What are we getting for this buck? What's the bang? What's the size of the bang?" and they want to push for the bigger size. [*sic*]

Gina's observation was consistent with Eugene van Erven's[6] findings that community theatre around the world is susceptible to the controlling interests of funders or sponsors and that those interests often focus on immediate, utilitarian, demonstrable results.

While fulfilling the responsibilities of recruiter, organizer, and manager is essential to success, the roles of artist and community builder are the primary roles for art practitioners to embrace. Gina's comments above also reflect one of the growing challenges of negotiating the role of artist. Some art practitioners experience devaluation as artists because of a focus on using the arts for functional purposes rather than appreciating art for its inherent value. Given the low status of the community artist's profession in the traditional art world and the de-funding of the arts in education, additional messages of devaluation can further challenge feelings of self-worth for art practitioners. Ralph the storyteller explains what he has seen in his career:

> To the extent that they can check off their to-do list, on that agenda [it] is not saying, "I'd like my kids to stretch and explore their imagination. I'd like them to play with crafting character or painting pictures with words." That's not down. So you show up and say, "Here, I've spent my life doing this; am I valuable to you?" And they go, "No, I don't see anything valuable to it. Oh, wait a minute. You can do something. Can you do African stories? Oh, so we can do Black Awareness Month. We can check off that. We've got to do that. Oh, you can help." So in community projects it seems like where you can get funding from is, "We want to reduce crime in the neighborhood. And so if we can get the kids who might end up in gangs to come into your community art project, then here, we'll give you $10,000." [*sic*]

Again, van Erven's findings from his international series of case studies on community theater concurred that "when it attracts funding at all, community theatre is usually only validated according to social development instead of aesthetic criteria, both in the north and in the south."[7] Thus, with sponsors focusing primarily on instrumental goals, artists often are faced with defending their aesthetic choices.

In negotiating the role as community artist, art practitioners also may struggle with the balance between facilitating and taking control. Making art that involves large numbers of people requires that art practitioners be clear in providing their artistic visions and be confident in making artistic decisions. However, a balance must also be struck between artistic vision and a community's creative expression.[8] Sometimes, the art practitioner may not like the community's ideas for personal, rather than professional, reasons. However, in those situations, it is important to remember that the authentic community-art process involves collectively working together and everyone has a say. It is critical that the art practitioner contribute his or her unique experience as an expert while not limiting the capacity for participants to contribute in the balance of an artist-driven, community-centered process.

Bridging Differences

With families, friends, and strangers coming together to make art, art practitioners help resolve differences among opinions, ideologies, and personalities. Given the cross-section of diversity that is typical in public school classrooms and was present in the community-art projects highlighted in this book, it seems only natural that participants sometimes disagree about issues or values. Art practitioners should demonstrate effective communication, listening, and conflict resolution skills to work with the dynamics that naturally occur among group members. For example, Caroline the choreographer described dealing with two boys who feared homosexuals and were faced with working with a lesbian during a production. Because Caroline facilitated a positive interaction to bridge their differences, the teenagers ultimately discovered that the lesbian was "just another woman and that's really cool." In the multimedia park project, we laid the foundation for success by teaching youth participants conflict resolution skills as a learning objective of the project.

Sometimes, art practitioners work with children and adults who have challenging life experiences such as mental and physical health issues. In one community-art project, the role of community builder demanded that an art practitioner overcome her own concerns about how to meet the needs of a girl with mental retardation and discover ways to include her effectively in the project. In another case, one of the artists was faced with integrating a teenage girl who would stop talking and roll on the floor in a fit while shouting aggressively at other youth. Fortunately, the outcomes of both challenging examples were positive for the art practitioners and the participants.

Bearing Responsibility for Success

Overwhelmingly, community artists in our case studies describe the community-art process as "an incredible amount of work." The variety of activities and roles that art practitioners fulfill may take hundreds of hours to implement successfully and may be exhausting, particularly in the community-based setting. Art practitioners are the focal points of the artistic activities and, as such, participants look to them for guidance, motivation, and role modeling. In addition, participants need a great deal of personal attention and follow-through, whether they are students or community members. Regardless of whether the personal attention involves support on a dance move, assistance with handling a tile, or any other type of assistance, art practitioners should treat the artistic contributions by each participant the way participants describe them: "individual treasures to be cherished." The variety of emotional and physical expectations of the role, combined with the experience of consistently being on stage as the starring community artist, may feel very demanding.

Keys to Success

The following are some helpful tips that we recommend artist practitioners keep in mind when facing challenges such as those described above:

- Maintain vision
- Persevere
- Balance focus and flexibility
- Collaborate
- Take the time to reflect and celebrate

As is true for any collective endeavor, keeping sight of the *vision* of a community-art project is essential to its success. Art practitioners must return community-art participants to the purposeful possibilities that brought the group together in order to maintain inspiration and involvement. In our case, throughout the multimedia park project we continually returned to the vision of a space for peace that would both transform the youth involved with the project and transform the community. Often we would talk about our belief in "what is possible," even in the face of numerous challenges. Keeping the possibility of the vision alive helped us focus on the big picture when day-to-day challenges and problems felt overwhelming.

Perseverance with transforming the challenges, or "relentless persistence" as Ralph the storyteller calls it, is another key to project success for both coordinators and participants, especially when working in underserved communities. When participants cast doubt that something as positive and creatively miraculous as community art is going to happen, the art practitioner must persevere. In the face of difficulties—even when the situation says "no"—the art practitioner must figure out ways to follow through. When challenges that could stop a community-art project arise, relentless persistence demands asking the strategic question: What will it take?

Being willing to ask what it will take to overcome difficulties compels an art practitioner to *balance focus and flexibility*. It is important to maintain vision while at the same time accept that the creative process or outcome may not look the way the art practitioner pictured it. Success in a community-based setting can be ensured by being flexible with what occurs and using unexpected events to forward progress toward the vision. This is the essence of creativity in collective action. For example, we thought the multimedia park project would be a six-month undertaking and that it would be created by one group of participants. We found after the project's first phase that we could not succeed with the existing resources and the original schedule, so we shifted our thinking about continuity requirements and participant demographics. As a result, we extended the timeline to nine months and adjusted the size of the finished project to fit the number of participants and the amount of time and money available.

Collaboration is not only inherent to community art but also invaluable for ensuring success. Whether collaboration means using existing resources found in the neighborhood or school, or effectively partnering with multiple project coordinators, a multiplicity of input sources is key for the creativity, balance, and accountability required for success. When sharing leadership, the involvement of coordinators can ebb and flow. One coordinator may take the lead on different elements while another takes a needed break from the project. This allows the project to continue without extreme burnout, which can be disastrous for any endeavor.

A final essential component for a successful experience is to build in time for *reflection and celebration*. Scheduling the space to debrief with key collaborators immediately after every workshop session or structured activity is helpful. Reflection is an important key to success because it provides the space to ask questions and share insights. By incorporating thoughtful responses to circumstances along the way, art practitioners ensure a positive process and outcome. With reflection, the community-art process can be embraced as a work of art itself, a masterpiece of communal proportion. As a masterpiece in the making, celebrating every accomplishment and lesson along the way is critical.

Notes

1. Howard S. Becker, *Art Worlds* (Berkeley: University of California Press, 1982).
2. Becker, *Art Worlds*.

3. Beth Krensky, "Going Beyond Zebra: A Middle School and Community-Based Arts Organization Collaborate for Change," *Education and Urban Society* 33, no. 4 (August 2001): 427–44.

4. E. Mahony, "Once Is Too Much," *Art Bulletin* (April/May1998): 17–18.

5. Maryo Ewell and Peter Ewell, "Planning for Grassroots Arts Development," *Arts in Society* 12, no. 1 (Summer 1975): 92–109.

6. Eugene Van Erven, *Community Theatre: Global Perspectives* (New York: Routledge, 2001).

7. Van Erven, *Community Theatre: Global Perspectives*, 254.

8. Mahony, "Once Is Too Much": 17–18.

CHAPTER FOUR

The Participants: Seeing the Power of Community Art

Community art provides people with a shared interest and a structured opportunity to interact, during which time participants discover the power of the arts to evoke new possibilities for personal and social life. Both the experience of making art and the outcome of the art itself have the power to compel openings for individual and collective change. This chapter summarizes existing research on those changes and highlights our findings about the transformative power of the arts to benefit individuals and communities that participate in community-art projects. As mentioned in chapter 2, our findings are drawn from research that spanned four years and involved 220 participants.

Individual Change

Research shows that imaginative exploration can have significant impacts on individuals. From the perspective of neuroscience, art activities are positively linked to cognitive development.[1] In the field of education, longitudinal research shows that participating in the arts is connected to higher academic achievement.[2] Indeed, data analyzed from the National Education Longitudinal Study (NELS) suggest that high school students involved in arts programming achieve better grades and score higher on standardized tests than uninvolved students.[3] Shirley Brice Heath and a team of researchers also examined the impact of community-art programs on the young people who attend them. They found that those who regularly attend arts-based programs "improve their academic standing, increase their abilities in self-assessment and motivation and raise their sense of the importance of planning and working for a positive future for themselves and their communities."[4] For children from fourth to eighth grade, Judith Burton, Robert Horowitz, and Hal Abeles found that those students who were involved in rich in-school arts programs demonstrated greater creativity, fluency, originality, and elaboration.[5] Sociologically, youth involved in the arts tend to be more likely to participate in positive social activities and to feel positively about themselves than those who are not participating in art activities.[6] All of these studies point to the potential for positive change that exists when individuals have opportunities to participate in arts-based programming. This study adds to that knowledge by demonstrating that the experience of doing community art contributes to the development of identity and efficacy for individuals.[7]

Self-Identity

Identity is the collection of ideas and feelings about oneself or one's group as a known entity; in essence, it is our sense of who we are and what we have to offer. Developing new skills and using them in a setting where participants creatively explore possibilities for themselves and their communities expands self-concept. Such skills as communication, leadership, conflict resolution, decision making, group dynamics, and public speaking are common lasting impacts. For example, one group of young people was failing in school, unable to spell or write well. During their community-art project, they learned literacy skills to craft poetry about their lives, and those abilities continued over time and affected their sense of themselves as writers and their success in school. Gina the storyteller witnessed continuing changes for a group of women who collaboratively wrote a play and then participated in the process of making role, costume, design, and production decisions. During the community-art project, she observed that the women became more assertive in their lives in response to oppressive circumstances. The skill of characterization allowed them to "pretend" to set boundaries in relationships, thereby setting healthier boundaries in real-life relationships. This was particularly true for a woman in her late thirties from an inner-city neighborhood who was in an abusive marriage and described herself as a "very timid" person. She said, "The dance class gave me the courage to take the next step, to realize that I needed to make some changes in my life." As a result of participating in the community-art project, she chose to leave the relationship. Gina also observed that the skill of exercising voice quality continued to enable participants to be more effective in work situations such as interviews and sales interactions.

During community art, the experience of developing new skills, including creative methods of self-expression, and practicing them while trying on roles within a supportive setting enables individuals to cultivate new dimensions of their identity, with the result that participants often experience a greater sense of self-worth. The following exchange among a group of women in the theater project illustrates some of the changes experienced as a result of doing community art:

> Maria: I was feeling worthless, like nothing; now I have self-confidence and self-worth.
>
> Marissa: We have been told that we were worth nothing, but when we come to school and talk to each other and share the good strength we see in each other, we recognize the qualities in each other and help (each other) really do something for [ourselves] and [our] kids. We just need encouragement.
>
> Regina: If I have pride, I can be proud for my daughter and she will be a better person.

Community art's unique potential for the exploration and discovery of possibilities leads many participants to envision themselves as contributors. The opportunity to engage in community art allows participants to see themselves in new roles such as "dancer" or "leader" that continue to affect how they define their capacities and roles beyond the community-art process. For example, a survey respondent shared that involvement in her first community-art project helped her see that she could be the coordinator in the next project in her neighborhood. In a classroom setting during the multimedia park project, small groups of seven or eight students worked with adult facilitators who were professional artists or designers. The access to professional artists not only allowed the students to get rigorous art training and critical feedback but also gave them access to the art world. While working and interacting with these various art and design professionals, they began to see and speak new possibilities for themselves as future web designers, architects, or artists.

Caroline the choreographer tells about another participant who significantly altered her identity and envisioned herself as a dancer:

> Annie, [when she] came in, she was very heavy with no self-esteem and really wanted to dance. And at the end of the year of our program she said, "You know, I want to audition for School of the Arts." And I said, "Go for it." And I really didn't know how she would do, but she got in. And she came back to me and I said, "Congratulations." And she said, "No, really I should congratulate you.

You're the one who gave me the courage to go do this and gave me the confidence that I could do this." And she's still there.

The technical skills developed in community art expand participants' abilities to express themselves creatively in meaningful and lasting ways. It is not uncommon for community art to spawn continued artistic involvement for participants who now see themselves as artists, as illustrated in the story about Annie. In our research, some participants chose to expand their capacities for creative expression by pursuing arts-related education as a result of their involvement, and others sought or were sought after for professional artistic opportunities. Community art gives participants an opportunity to learn and grow artistically, which otherwise may be limited by the cost of arts programs or the cuts in arts education throughout public schools.

In addition, when participants are youth, the mentorship and learning that take place provide an avenue for creatively exploring and expressing who they are in new ways. Our research showed that young people typically gained a means of expression they did not have in other areas of their lives. Community art provided a chance for them to voice their thoughts and feelings: to share what they believe, hope, and fear. CBAE also provides opportunities for participants to find success in the arts when they may not have been successful in other areas of their lives.

Self-Efficacy

The evolution of identity is an empowering stepping stone for heightened levels of efficacy among participants. Self-efficacy is the belief in oneself and one's abilities to influence change in surrounding environments,[8] or, as one participant described after his community-art experience, believing "that if you put your mind to something, you can go all the way with it." Efficacy emerged as confidence among participants in their abilities to accomplish something both during and after the activities of art making. As different skills were acquired and physical objects were created, many participants shifted from not believing they could create anything to seeing their power to act and to influence. In the case of the multimedia park project, the development of self-efficacy enabled participants to interact with public officials, make presentations to community members, and advocate for the project. The youth came to see themselves as people who could effect change. Many of the young people talked about how they could create something like the multimedia park, despite other peoples' disbelief. One youth reported that her grandparents had said, "Oh, no, you probably didn't do that," and she replied, "'Yeah, I did!' It just made 'em sorta proud." Another youth said,

"It will make the parents and other people's parents [think] that we're responsible and when we put our minds to something we can do it" as a result of being involved.

The participants also exhibited efficacy by taking ownership of the park and their community. As the multimedia park project was under way, many young people began patrolling the area as a security measure. During the landscaping phase, a vandal uprooted nine newly planted trees; three of the participants discovered this and enlisted the help of parents to replant the trees. Other participants patrolled the area to prevent people from drinking in the park. One youth tells about taking action with another community-art participant when neighborhood teens began writing on a newly painted picnic shelter:

> We saw them writing and we said, "You guys know we spent a lot of time on this, and you guys can't ruin it already. They just look at us and keep writing and then we left. We came back and they were still doing it and we go, "You guys better stop!" and then they left. [*sic*]

This quote exemplifies the belief that action could be taken to influence change in the park. The idea that the participants could "transform and remake" their world was discussed by many of the participants. Some young people noted how designing the park and helping the community made them believe that they could accomplish other things in their neighborhood and beyond. One girl said that she could "help all the people. I could grow trees . . . I could grow flower seeds and tree seeds and a lot of different things." Another participant decided that she could solve future problems in her community. She said, "If any problems have happened and people started moving out, I'd be really disappointed, and I'd have to try to find out what the problem was and try to solve it somehow." In addition, several youth who had initially feared public speaking made several presentations on behalf of their community, one of which had an audience of seventy people. John, a thirteen-year-old, talks about how being part of the project helped him conquer his fear of public speaking:

> I kind of conquered my fear of speech and talking. I hated talking in front of anybody, the crowds. I had a fear of speech and I made three or four speeches, which put me in a better position to give speeches in front of crowds of people. And then the Lions Club and when the newspaper people were there and I had that big speech I did that pretty good. . . . Now I give speeches in school, read off announcements. [*sic*]

A reporter from the local newspaper concurred with John's observations over the period of months that the participants were involved with the community-art project:

> A sense of empowerment and a sense of accomplishment are two of the benefits that I have noticed. . . . It gave them confidence, some of them leadership skills. When they talk to me they're confident. They're not shy like they used to be.

The youth also planned and presented an overview of the community-art project to the local city council. They arrived prepared with visual and written descriptions of their plans as well as charts that portrayed community feedback about the project, and they requested an annual day to honor their neighborhood. As a result, the city council passed a resolution to institute such a day with a name consistent with the theme of their community-art project, and the council members unanimously voted to grant the two participating sixth-grade classes a "Certificate of Good Citizenship." One city council member said, "This is what education should be about. These students have exemplified what it means to be model citizens."

The following is a model case study of a community-art participant who illustrates the potential for positive change in the areas of self-identity and self-efficacy by developing her expertise as an artist, seeing herself as a contributor, and demonstrating leadership in her community.

Amber's Story

At the beginning of the multimedia park project, twelve-year-old Amber would rarely talk to adults or other youth, and when she did speak, she whispered inaudibly or with a shake of the head. She often would hunch silently in her chair or roll on the floor during workshop activities. This behavior was interspersed with violent outbreaks when she would hit or shout at other youth or workshop leaders. Rae, one of the art practitioners, describes her this way:

> She would sit crouched on the floor, huddled down with her face on the ground, and not raise it up for a half an hour. And then, all of the sudden, just explode and storm or stomp away. . . . She'd act very primal in some ways with her outbursts and she'd hit.

When Rae started attending the workshops to help the youth create ceramic tiles for a walkway, Amber would not speak to her. Rae was persistent in her support of Amber as an artist, however, and they initiated a friendship. The patience, compassion, creative skills, and teaching brought by the art practitioner created an environment for Amber "to express her individual ideas, personality, and beauty by allowing her to communicate when words failed her. Through her artwork, Amber was able to discover herself and realize her potential for self-expression." Whenever Rae was on site, Amber worked by her side. Amber became the resident expert in handmade ceramic tiles. As a result, Rae observed, "With a newfound sense of confidence and empowerment, Amber developed relationships with her peers and the community toward becoming a community youth leader."

Amber had indeed started interacting with her peers and the other project leaders, volunteers, and artists in more responsive and positive ways. She had conversations with people (as opposed to her earlier nonverbal communication) and had positive things to say about the art (in contrast to her previous negative comments about most things and people). A number of youth and adults from the neighborhood who had not previously been involved in the project began to help out or attend special gatherings because Amber had invited them to participate. Amber also organized a group of neighborhood youth to be on "trash patrol" for the area. During post-project interviews, numerous young people credited Amber for their involvement in the project, saying, "Amber told me about it" or "Amber made me come." She also was the primary organizer of a surprise birthday celebration for one of the volunteers. Amber confidently made a presentation about the tile entrance art piece at the unveiling and spoke with reporters and adult attendees during the event. Amber's story reflects the power of community art to foster significant changes for individuals who participate in the imaginative experience uniquely available in the free space of art.

Social Change

Dewey[9] argued that the arts can call a community to its future by portraying a vision of a unified collective life and serving as the instrument to create that vision. He asserted that the arts are "marvelous aids in the creation of such a life."[10] Indeed, research on the arts reveals that the arts provide natural, unique openings for various levels of social change as a result of the dynamic interaction inherent in the artistic experience. Lev Vygotsky, Russian psychologist and author of *The Psychology of Art*, explained that art actively engages people by compelling a response and, as a result of its active engagement, "forces us to strive beyond our life toward all that lies beyond it."[11] Research and writings on the transformative nature of the arts at the community level have identified the positive impacts of the arts on building community and addressing community problems.[12] In addition, the role of the arts and artists as instruments of social change has been seen in research linking community art and community development and showing art as a catalyst for systemic change.[13]

Our research indicates that the creation of community art is instrumental in fostering new possibilities for participating groups. Indeed, our study demonstrates that community art has the ability to build solidarity, develop and reinforce collective identity, and foster collective efficacy.[14] In addition, the artwork itself serves as a symbolic referent for the communities that receive installation pieces. The overwhelmingly positive meaning of the artistic symbolism is significant not only because of the duration of its impact but also because of its power to continue to inspire community possibilities. As Cohen explained, "People's experience and understanding of their community . . . resides in their orientation to their symbolism."[15]

Community Art

Our findings indicate that personal pieces or permanent installations of community art are symbolically significant for participants because of their aesthetic appeal, their legacies, and their memories. Participants of this study found their works of community art "astonishingly beautiful" and "aesthetically pleasing." Their presence as "a mark made by people in the community" was described as "welcoming" and "invigorating." In addition to bringing beauty and pleasure to participants, the artworks represented positive contributions to the community seen by participants as "a piece of me that will be history and will be shared with future generations." For example, Jeannie, a forty-five-year-old European-American from the mural project, explained, "The best part for me is the legacy, and I find whenever I'm going by one of those parks and I'm with somebody that doesn't know anything about it or doesn't know that we did that, I have this huge desire to make them know." A thirty-eight-year-old Chicana mother commented that the art was "a remembrance of working together with my children." For a seventy-seven-year-old retired woman, "It makes me aware that nothing is impossible and that people have talents that we would never have guessed." The art symbolized the meaning and significance of their experiences as a community.

Works of community art often continue to impact a community because they demarcate community, change the landscape of communal space, and provide gathering places to eat, play, and visit with other community members. Permanent installations appear to have a greater likelihood of inspiring lasting community results because of their symbolic presence as "third places," which are the "public places that host the regular, voluntary, informal, and happily anticipated gatherings of individuals beyond the realms of home and work."[16] As one participant described, the art sends a message "that the world can come visit." In the multimedia park project, an art practitioner explains that the art was:

> an ongoing reminder of what it took and it was a created community effort. So it's an ongoing reminder of that and the message of peace in the community. It also is just so much more joyous with the colors and the images than the park would be if it was just structures. It calls to people. Structures call to people one way, like come play on me. The art calls to people in saying come interact with me, come understand, come think about or enjoy.

For participants, the art was an expression of community importance, permanence, and continuity. In most cases, the community art remained intact over time because of the respect it was accorded as a symbolic referent of the community.

Sense of Community

Another important outcome for groups of participants in community art is the development and enhancement of a sense of community. The strongest evidence for change from our findings points to the emergence of solidarity. The data reveal that connections among neighbors, friends, and even family are enhanced in enduring ways for participants and that community pride remains over time. The safe, lighthearted setting of community-art projects gives participants the opportunity to work together in ways that allow them to discover new connections and deepen existing ones. In terms of relationships, participants demonstrated warmth, openness, and mutuality consistent with a sense of traditional neighborliness.[17] The community-art experience fostered a sense of connection and fellowship, altering feelings of isolation and disconnection for many. Participants found that they were more comfortable interacting with strangers and acquaintances in their neighborhoods and were more patient with others in their community since completing their community-art project.

Participants discussed how their experiences working with strangers, friends, and family while doing community art contributed positively to the quality of their interpersonal relationships years after project completion. Barriers had been broken down and openings had been created as a result of coming together. During the process, participants learned that "being different from others was not a bad thing." Shelley, a participant in the mural project, observes, "The kids got to see how the elders see the circus [referring to the mural project]. [It's] a diverse representation of a shared experience." Racial and generational gaps were bridged by the opportunities to meet and learn about each other in the safe, supportive free space of community art. Teens shared about how adults helped them succeed. Older children mentored younger participants throughout all three projects.

Participants also established lasting friendships while engaged in CBAE. Bernadino, a thirteen-year-old Latino boy, said that he met his best friend while working on the project. Lupita, a sixty-two-year-old Hispanic woman, observes, "I found a lot of understanding people. . . . We start out as friends and become family. We have one family at home and one at [the art project]." An adult survey respondent states:

> I still see these people and [am] developing friendships with them. There have been several projects and time has passed so I know more people! I can say I feel more connected to people, but the project was not the only "cause" because time has passed and my connections have deepened.

Resoundingly, pride in being a member of the community was an aspect of solidarity that endured for participants and nonparticipants in many of the project sites. Respondents spoke about their connection to the neighborhood, the art itself, and their involvement in making the art, and they said they would take friends to see the art or would acknowledge their role in creating it when speaking with others. Jeannie, a member from the mural project, describes it as "part of my life. For me, it's like a little badge of honor. It's an accomplishment. It represents a lot of goodness in my life, creating something of lasting beauty in our neighborhood."

Once permanent works of community art are installed, an expanded sense of pride and ownership develops in the wider community. In our research, nonparticipants frequently expressed pride in the art, in knowing those who were involved in its development, or in the community itself. Adrienne the painter offers one example:

> I was at [the local middle school] recruiting for [my organization] a few weeks ago [two years after completion] and we were showing [community-art project] examples and . . . there was actually a little boy who pointed to a tile and said, "Yeah, I painted that tile." And he hadn't been involved in [my organization] since then, but he was really excited, and definitely had a lot of pride in the project. And now, with the kids who are coming to the drop-in center who were not a part of that project, I sense this kind of respect and admiration for what the [community-art project] kids had done. They look through pictures of the project and say, "Oh, yeah, I've been there." And I tell them that kids

> from [my organization] designed and built it and they say something like, "Oh, yeah, I know them," or "I've been there," and they are just proud to be associated with the project.

The mother of a young boy who participated in the multimedia park project expressed that pride had not previously been present in her low-income neighborhood but had emerged as a result of the project. In her opinion, the community-art project brought the community together around something very positive that their children had initiated and in a way they had not experienced before.

Collective Identity

Beyond the sense of community, those who participated in the community-art projects during this study demonstrated the power of art to develop and reinforce collective identity. With community art, "a way of speaking of an expanded community . . . takes shape when diverse people, speaking as who, and not what, they are, come together in both speech and action to constitute something in common among themselves."[18] Particularly, cohesion around culture and sense of place were constituted as the collective identities among the projects in our study. In addition, the artwork tended to take on and maintain a defining role for the collective as a symbolic referent for identity. For those coming together in community art, a desire existed to unite across differences, whether ethnic or generational. With the mural project, for example, African-American, Asian-American, European-American, Hispanic, Native-American, and Vietnamese neighborhood residents discovered a unifying theme in neighborhood history to define themselves as a cohesive group. With the multimedia park project, participants united around a common interests in peace and play, and with the theater project, diverse generations celebrated a common cultural history.

The identity of a sense of place appeared to be particularly resilient for participants. In the following focus group interaction, Doris, a high-school-educated, seventy-six-year-old woman, articulates the sense of connection that many continued to feel:

> My dad was an army colonel, so I always moved around when I was a kid and I would live like a year and a half one place, maybe three years in one place and so I'm really not from any place, you know, I've always moved around. And this is the first time that I've lived a long time in one place. And so for me, when I moved here and I had my children, it was real important to get a sense of community. And by doing [community art], I feel like I'm putting down

> roots for the first time in my life. Even though I may move again sometime, really now I kind of belong in a place because of this. [*sic*]

Belinda, a thirty-eight-year-old Navajo woman, also talks about an enduring sense of place for her children who participated:

> My kids are very artistic but this was something that, my oldest said that she has something in [the neighborhood] that she will always remember [the neighborhood] by. She made something that if she happens to move away from here that she will always have in her heart, the ceramic tiles. They come back and say, "That's what I did. Even if I become real old, walking with a cane, I can say, 'This is what I made.'" [*sic*]

Collective Efficacy

Similar to self-efficacy, collective efficacy can be seen as a collectively held belief in the capacity of one's group to effect change. Our research found that cohering around commonalities helped to mobilize communities and to inspire people to connect with other residents and organizations about issues of local concern. Specifically, participants discovered shared concerns such as isolation, cultural differences, financial hardship, family responsibilities, gangs, and violence.

Many participants maintained a belief in their community and willingness to play a role in shaping their local environment. Marco, a seventh-grade, Mexican-American youth, stated during a focus group that he thought community art improved community life because "when people create art, they are proud of what they have created and then more likely to work on bettering other parts of the community and less likely to damage or trash places like parks." Gina, based on her experience as a community artist, substantiates Marco's belief:

> I also think they're not only essential, [community-art projects] are necessary to a community. And this comes out of my work as a nurse, as a health care worker, and as an artist, that a community is not healthy just because I can say all the children are immunized and cancer rates are down. There's a wonderful poem that I've lived by for years, at least thirty. And it's called "Bread and Roses." And it's a poem that was written about women textile workers. . . . And essentially what it says is that we don't live by bread alone. We need the roses, too. And just because another neighborhood can afford boulevards of beautifully planted flowers doesn't mean that a poorer neighborhood less appreciates the beauty of those geraniums and pansies. And you can be free of cancer, but if you're still fearful because no one has touched on that emotional piece, then

> you're not healthy. And that's where the roses as a symbol come in. And that's where art comes in. And maybe in a poorer neighborhood, we put our geraniums in empty coffee cans. And when you start moving things around in this creative process, that community becomes healthier, more assertive, and . . . they start keeping their medical appointments better. I saw it. They then stand up for their rights.

Both Marco's predictions and Gina's observations were validated by the responses of many different participants who were more motivated to serve their communities. The mural project resulted in residents' "working hard to keep the neighborhood safe and clean. The artwork gives everyone more incentive to accomplish this goal." Some people reported that they continued to interact with the neighborhood organization that sponsored the community-art project or to volunteer in their community after completing the project. A seventy-four-year-old female survey respondent wrote that there was continuing "improvement in all aspects" of neighborhood life as a result of the community-art project and believed that the children's playground was "more safe and crime free" as a result of increased community involvement.

Clearly, the transformative power of making art and the outcome of the art itself benefit individuals and communities that participate in community art. At both individual and collective levels, the artwork and identification with its symbolic power tend to endure. For groups, a sense of community, identity, and efficacy are positive impacts that can be expected, and for individuals, self-identity and self-efficacy are positive results that are typical outcomes to add to the success indicators of community cultural development. Table 4.1 encapsulates the findings from the field of research on art.

Table 4.1. Research on the Power of the Arts

Area of Impact	*Type of Impact*
The Arts and Individual Change	• Promote positive cognitive development • Increase academic achievement • Develop greater motivation • Cultivate greater creativity, fluency, originality, and elaboration • Increase participation in positive social activities and positive feelings about oneself • Develop identity and self-efficacy
The Arts and Social Change	• Foster community development • Build a sense of community • Develop collective identity and efficacy • Catalyze systemic change

Notes

1. Sharon Begley, "Your Child's Brain," *Newsweek*, February 19, 1996, 55–62; James Shreeve, "Music of the Hemispheres," *Discover*, October 1996, 90–100.

2. Judith Burton, Robert Horowitz, and Hal Abeles, "Learning in and through the Arts: Curricular Implications," in *Champions of Change: The Impact of the Arts on Learning*, ed. Edward B. Fiske (Washington, D.C.: The Arts Education Partnership and the President's Committee on the Arts and Humanities, 1999); James S. Catterall, Richard Chapleau, and John Iwanaga, "Involvement in the Arts and Human Development: General Involvement and Intense Involvement in Music and Theatre Arts," in *Champions of Change: The Impact of the Arts on Learning*, ed. Edward B. Fiske (Washington, D.C.: The Arts Education Partnership and the President's Committee on the Arts and Humanities, 1999); Shirley Brice Heath and Adelma Roach, "Imaginative Activity: Learning in the Arts During the Non-School Hours," in *Champions of Change: The Impact of the Arts on Learning*, ed. Edward B. Fiske (Washington, D.C.: The Arts Education Partnership and the President's Committee on the Arts and Humanities, 1999).

3. James S. Catterall, "Involvement in the Arts and Success in Secondary School," *Americans for the Arts Monograph Series* 1, no. 9 (December 1997/January 1998); James Catterall, Richard Chapleau, and John Iwanaga, "Involvement in the Arts and Human Development: General Involvement and Intense Involvement in Music and Theatre Arts."

4. Shirley Brice Heath has collaborated with other researchers to examine community youth arts programs and the impact on the young people who attend them. This research has found that young people who regularly attend arts-based programs "improve their academic standing, increase their abilities in self-assessment and motivation, and raise their sense of the importance of planning and working for a positive future for themselves and their communities." Some of the research is found in the following publications: Shirley Brice Heath, Elisabeth Soep, and Adelma Roach, "Living the Arts through Language and Learning: A Report on Community-Based Youth Organizations," *Americans for the Arts Monographs* 2, no. 7 (November 1998): 1–20; Shirley Brice Heath and Milbrey McLaughlin, eds., *Identity and Inner-City Youth: Beyond Ethnicity and Gender* (New York: Teachers College Press, 1993).

5. Burton, Horowitz, and Abeles, "Learning in and through the Arts: Curricular Implications," 35–46.

6. Debra Holloway and Beth Krensky, "The Arts, Urban Education, and Social Change," *Education and Urban Society* 33, no. 4 (August 2001): 354–65.

7. Seana Lowe, "Creating Community: Art for Community Development," *Journal of Contemporary Ethnography* 29, no. 3 (June 2000): 357–86.

8. Viktor Gecas, "The Social Psychology of Self-Efficacy," *Annual Review of Sociology* 15 (August 1989); Benjamin Barber, *An Aristocracy of Everyone: The Politics of Education and the Future of America* (Oxford, New York, and Toronto: Oxford University Press, 1992).

9. John Dewey, *Art as Experience* (New York: Minton, Balch & Company, 1934).

10. Dewey, *Art as Experience*, 81.

11. Lev S. Vygotsky, *The Psychology of Art* (Cambridge, Mass.: The MIT Press, 1925/1971), 253.

12. Edward Brown II, "Community-Based Art in Philadelphia," *Art Papers* 18, no. 3 (May–June 1994): 38–40; Dale Cyphert, "Pleasure, Pedagogy, and Oppression in the Heartland," *Text and Performance Quarterly* 18, no. 1 (1998): 27–49; Susan Perlstein, "Intergenerational Arts: Cultural Continuity and Community Cohesion," *Journal of Aging and Identity* 2, no. 4 (1997): 273–84; Seymour Simmons III, "Creating Community Through Art: Two Research Project Reviews," *The Journal of Social Theory in Art Education*, no. 18 (1998): 59–76; Helen Wositzky, "Out of the Ashes, a Community Responds: The Dandenong Ranges Bushfires," *Australian Journal of Emergency Management* (Winter 1988): 17–20; David Fisher, "Public Art and Public Space," *Soundings* 79, no. 1–2 (Spring–Summer 1996): 41–57; Javier Stanzioloa, *Arts, Government and Community Revitalization* (Sydney: Ashgate, 1999).

13. Bernie Jones, "The Community Artist as Community Development Catalyst: An Evaluation of a Pilot Project," *Journal of the Community Development Society* 19, no. 1 (1988): 37–50; P. Overton, "Arts Development in Rural and Small Towns," *Connections Quarterly* (Winter 1987): 12ff.

14. Seana Lowe, "Creating Community: Art for Community Development."

15. Anthony Cohen, *The Symbolic Construction of Community* (New York: Tavistock Publications, 1985).

16. Ray Oldenburg, *The Great Good Places: Cafés, Coffee Shops, Community Centers, Beauty Parlors, General Stores, Bars, Hang Outs, and How They Get You Through the Day* (New York: Paragon, 1989), 16.

17. Arthur Vidich and Joseph Bensman, *Small Town in Mass Society* (Princeton: Princeton University Press, 1968).

18. Maxine Greene, *Releasing the Imagination: Essays on Education, the Arts, and Social Change* (San Francisco: Jossey-Bass, 1995), 155.

CHAPTER FIVE

The Theory behind the Practice

As chapter 4 illustrates, the arts positively impact individuals and communities. Art uniquely inspires us as human beings to see creative possibilities for our world and ourselves. In these openings or free spaces of artistic potential, we are connected to our shared humanity and called to fulfill our human need to create. Given the outcomes from stepping into those free spaces of community art, it naturally follows to ask how and why such change happens. This chapter presents the theory behind the practice of community art. Drawing from educational, psychological, and sociological theory, we explain why community art affects participants in such distinct and profound ways.

Understanding the Collective Impacts

To understand why community art fosters a sense of community, collective identity, and collective efficacy, we look to theories of ritual and social constructivism, drawing from Erich Fromm, Lev Vygotsky, Pierre Bourdieu, and Howard S. Becker to explain the relatively complex phenomenon. Social psychologist Erich Fromm believed that, for humanity to be healthy and productive, people must explore their world artistically. He defined art as the expression of one's understanding of the world by one's senses and bemoaned the loss of shared artistic experiences in the modern world. Fromm referred to collective art as a ritual essential to building a sane society: "Collective art is shared; it permits man [*sic*] to feel one with others in a meaningful, rich, productive way."[1] He asserted that collective art is a necessary part of life because it fulfills a fundamental human need to interact with the world in creative and meaningful ways. Building on Fromm, collective art is critical to transforming "an atomistic into a communitarian society"[2] because it fosters a sense of interconnection and community by providing the essential elements of a ritual framework for social interaction.[3] Community art compels personal and social transformation by uniquely combining the change process found in rituals with the power of art, both to symbolize the change that occurs and to inspire the opening for that change. Community art is considered a ritual because of its capacity to demarcate change in society and to reflect an individual's relationship to his or her group and the world outside the group. As such, rituals have the distinct capacity to "create a communality even among a group of people for whom the structures of community have been severely diminished."[4]

Another early examination of the phenomenon of art as a social experience was conducted by psychologist Lev Vygotsky in 1925. According to Vygotsky, art contains the essence of our humanity. He believed that the aesthetic experience is a high "psychic activity" distinguished from other human experiences by the level of imagination involved for the maker and viewer. For Vygotsky, art unites feeling and imagination because the interactive process of experiencing it demands synergistic creativity. Vygotsky theorizes that:

> Art is the social within us, and even if its action is performed by a single individual, it does not mean that its essence is individual. . . . Art is the social technique of emotion, a tool of society which brings the most intimate and personal aspects of our being into the circle of social life.[5]

This thread between the emotional and social allows the experience of doing and viewing art to have significance in the larger arena of social life. Vygotsky explains, "Art requires a reply"[6] by eliciting interaction and, as a result of its active engagement, "forces us to strive beyond our life toward all that lies beyond it."[7] Community art is therefore a natural and unique opening for various levels of social communication, which in turn acts as a springboard for social change.

In a related but distinct line of thinking, philosopher John Dewey explored art's inherent quality of cultural symbolism. According to Dewey, "art speaks an idiom that conveys what cannot be said in another language."[8] The unique language of art allows participants to explore their visions for their community and declare those visions in the form of public visual statements for others to view and interact with. From Dewey's perspective, art both represents and is given by the community that is its context, and it is therefore intrinsically linked to social change. Hence, the power of community art lies in its ability to be both a context for creating a sense of community and a symbol representing that community's identity and its possible future.

For participants, community art uniquely allows creators and viewers to envision better futures and opens possibilities for individual and collective efficacy, because "only imaginative vision elicits the possibilities that are woven within the textures of the actual. The first stirrings of dissatisfaction and the first intimations of a better future are always found in works of art."[9] Creativity and imagination allow one to escape hegemonic thinking and to create possibilities by moving beyond perceived boundaries, which can free one to build, make, create, and re-create the world.[10] Issue-oriented CBAE, in particular, provides a variety of practices that support participants in developing awareness of and engagement in social and political issues in ways that enable participants to envision new realities beyond the issues. Such envisioning, coupled with a sense of collective efficacy, can lead to societal transformation.

In 1982, sociologist Howard S. Becker explored the nature of art by identifying the interactions involved in its production and consumption, or what theorists call its "social construction." According to Becker, the pattern of complex cooperative activity involved in making and valuing art is an "art world." He then defined art as a collective action that involves an intricate series of interactions, beginning with the artistic idea itself. Necessary steps include the creation and distribution of the artistic materials required to bring the idea to fruition, the exchange of resources in securing the materials, and all support activities required to create art.[11] Similar to Vygotsky, Becker theorized that art inherently requires a social response. In his analysis, the artist serves as the center of a network of collective action, and the majority of the cooperation that occurs is based on socially constructed normative agreements, including agreements that define the fundamentals for "good" artwork.

The production and consumption of art as a social construction were also examined by sociologist Pierre Bourdieu. Beginning with the premise that art is a social fact given its aesthetic status by a particular collection of activities and actors, Bourdieu focused his analysis on the historical institution of the "cultured habitus," or norms of valuation and stratification, and the "artistic field." Similar to Becker's concept of the art world, the cultured habitus and artistic field together serve as the foundation for any art's existence as a "symbolic object endowed with meaning and value."[12] Bourdieu broadened the analysis by adding that any significance bestowed on a work of art is situated in a particular historical context and is constituted by a viewer who has been trained in that time period by appropriate privileged opportunities to see the object as a work of art. He also noted that there is a social process involved in creating the "creator" or artist to be the expert authorized to produce valued objects, and he identified the importance that a specialized language plays in constructing the social reality of art worlds. Bourdieu critiqued the elitism of the traditional art world as culturally constructed by the hegemony of the ruling class.

Understanding that the role of professional artist is socially constructed to be an expert with specialized language for the role is key to explaining community art's power to impact participants. From a sociological perspective, the community artist represents the institution of the art world and is legitimized by society to define the norms of creative interaction and the standards for artistic expression. Applied to the construct of community art as a ritual, with the power of ritual to invoke and demarcate change, the community artist can be thought of as having an authority role comparable to that of a ritual elder or specialist facilitating the ritual. Consequently, the community artist is normatively authorized to manage the essential elements of a ritual framework, such as the mood and the focus on community building and art making.[13] The community artist also uses the specialized language of constructing art worlds to declare an objective artistic reality that participants trust and internalize when redefining a sense of community or self. Consequently, the community artist's role as a specialist facilitating community art is critical to fulfilling community art's change potential.

Understanding the Individual Impacts

In community art, the involvement of the socially validated role of artist legitimates the art making. As Becker explains, "Artists are some sub-group of the world's participants who, by common agreement, possess a special gift, therefore make a unique and indispensable contribution to the work, and thereby make it art."[14] From a traditional perspective, it is indeed a "radical, transformative act"[15] to blur the boundaries of the art world by bringing high-art status to a popular setting in a capacity that validates art making by untrained artists. Understanding the impacts of the idea of blurring identities can be furthered by sociologist Erving Goffman,[16] whose work proposes that one's identity arises out of interaction with others relative to structural, historical, and physical context factors. His dramaturgical model is based on the premise that people are actors on the stage of life playing to an audience. The actor's role is shaped through interaction with others as well as by the actor's own sense of his or her personal being and how he or she wishes to enact the role. Goffman asserts that "appearance" and "manner," which are elements of one's "front," also shape the interaction: "'Appearance' may be taken to refer to those stimuli which function at the time to tell us of the performer's social statuses."[17] Appearance comprises one's dress and props, including clothes, house, posture, expressions, and gestures. It serves to communicate one's status, gender, age, personal commitments, and occupation. "'Manner' may be taken to refer to those stimuli which function at the time to warn us of the interaction role the performer will expect to play in the oncoming situation."[18]

If an actor's role is shaped through interaction with others, one way to alter one's sense of identity or social position is through providing possible roles for one to explore with the appropriate support for cultivating appearance and cuing manner. During art making and community building inside this free space, participants can explore new identities and discover new possibilities for themselves. Indeed, anthropologist and educator Ann Locke Davidson asserts that because such external forces as "familial socialization, cultural practices, or the perception of historical circumstances by group members"[19] can leave little room for one to transform or shift identity, transforming identity requires relationships and practices that allow for "alternative identities" to exist. These alternative identities, which represent identities other than the one a person has or is destined for, provide possible lives that a person can choose to act out. Davidson suggests that alternative identities offer something new for one to strive to become.[20] Community art uniquely provides a free space where participants can envision possibilities for themselves beyond the realm of what already exists.[21] During art making and community building inside this free space, participants experience new roles authenticated by the community-art process: "The arts provide ways for individuals to give voice to or depict their experiences, to try on new identities or perspectives, and even to visualize, articulate, or act out the impossible."[22]

The opportunity to explore new identities is particularly salient for young participants. Vygotsky helps us understand how young people are affected by theorizing that development occurs through social interaction and depends on the people and activities in a child's environment. Learning occurs based upon what one has access to and is permitted to learn as well as on how much one is assisted in the process.[23] Vygotzky proposes that the zone of proximal development represents the distance between one's real level of development (as determined by independent problem solving) and one's potential level of development (as determined through problem solving with an adult or more capable peer). Developmental shifts that lead to higher mental processes occur through assisted learning, which consists of conversations and interactions with more capable others. Through assisted learning, one can move developmentally along a learning continuum from novice to assisted performance and, finally, to expert.

Given that cognitive development occurs through social interaction, community-art projects provide settings where young people can receive assisted learning through interactions with educators, artists, and other youth and adult "experts" in various fields. CBAE provides an opportunity for young participants to reach their potential levels of development as active, involved members of their community by providing a setting that is inherently open to change and predicated on mutual respect and interaction. The movement along the continuum is supported by hands-on experience that gives young people access to new knowledge, which, in turn, helps them to enhance emerging skills: "The zone of proximal development defines those functions that have not yet matured but are in the process of maturation, functions that will mature tomorrow but are currently in an embryonic state. These functions could be termed the 'buds' or 'flowers' of development rather than the 'fruits' of development."[24] CBAE is an authentic experience that provides the practice, resources, and assistance to develop the capacities necessary for success.

Educational scholar Barbara Rogoff also views development as a "process of transformation of participation"[25] that occurs as children participate and change responsibilities in various activities that exist within a sociocultural context. Within this context, young people develop as they interact with others in a cultural community. This type of community is defined as a community of participation, where "people assist each other in learning to be responsible, making choices and solving problems in ways that fit their own needs, while coordinating with those of others and with group functioning."[26] One hallmark of a community of participation is cooperative learning, similar to assisted learning, where young participants see each other as resources and collaborators rather than as competitors. In this type of participation structure, young people take on an apprenticeship role where they are able to develop competence through practice. Rogoff suggests that an individual develops competence through practice in community or institutional settings, in interpersonal situations with others, and in personal ways through participation and reflection.[27]

Such a framework supports the value of role making and role taking within communities of participation like CBAE, where participants move from peripheral to central positions of power. This possible shifting of power has implications for the development of self-efficacy. In particular, historically silenced groups may develop a sense of self-efficacy by taking on new roles during community art. As they gain skills and confidence, the participants accept new roles that, in turn, help them move along the continuum from novice to expert as well as move from peripheral to more central positions of power. Community-art projects are distinct communities of participation that develop individual identity and self-efficacy through role taking and assisted learning.

Conclusion

This chapter concludes section I by explaining the theory behind the practice that produces results like those illustrated in chapter 4. Community art is a collective, creative process that positively impacts individuals and groups by providing essential opportunities for cultural and personal expression. Whether being used to meet educational objectives, to create openings for positive change, or to satisfy artistic yearnings, community art is a transformative experience that has the distinct capacity to enhance the lives of those involved. In the following chapters, we provide detailed case studies of artistic media that are particularly compatible for implementing CBAE, including murals, graphics, photography, video, and dance. The case studies in section 2 are intended to illustrate the community-art process, highlighting essential steps and offering helpful resources. As you read, we invite you to imagine what possibilities of communal proportion might arise if you implement the framework presented in this book.

Notes

1. Erich Fromm, *The Sane Society* (New York: Holt, Rinehart & Winston, 1955), 302.
2. Erich Fromm, *The Sane Society*, 303.
3. Seana Lowe, "The Art of Community Transformation," *Education and Urban Society* 33, no. 4 (August 2001): 457–71.
4. Anthony Cohen, *The Symbolic Construction of Community* (New York: Tavistock Publications, 1985), 53.
5. Lev S. Vygotsky, *The Psychology of Art* (Cambridge, Mass.: The MIT Press, 1925/1971), 249.
6. Vygotsky, *The Psychology of Art*, 252.
7. Vygotsky, *The Psychology of Art*, 253.
8. John Dewey, *Art as Experience* (New York: Minton, Balch & Company, 1934), 106.

9. Dewey, *Art as Experience*, 346.

10. David E. Purpel, *The Moral and Spiritual Crisis in Education: A Curriculum for Justice and Compassion in Education* (New York; Westport, Conn.; and London: Bergin and Garvey, 1989).

11. Howard S. Becker, *Art Worlds* (Berkeley: University of California Press, 1982).

12. Pierre Bourdieu, *The Field of Cultural Production* (New York: Columbia University Press, 1993), 257.

13. Seana Lowe, "The Art of Community Transformation," 457–71.

14. Becker, *Art Worlds*, 35.

15. Robin Pacific, "This Is Not a Benetton Ad: The Theory of Community Art," *MIX* 23, no. 3 (Winter 1997–1998): 40.

16. Erving Goffman, *The Presentation of Self in Everyday Life* (Garden City, N.Y.: Doubleday and Company, Inc., 1959).

17. Goffman, *The Presentation of Self in Everyday Life*, 24.

18. Goffman, *The Presentation of Self in Everyday Life*, 24.

19. Ann Locke Davidson, *Making and Molding Identity in Schools: Student Narratives on Race, Gender, and Academic Engagement* (Albany: SUNY Press, 1996), 3.

20. Davidson, *Making and Molding Identity in Schools*.

21. Dewey, *Art as Experience*; Maxine Greene, *Releasing the Imagination: Essays on Education, the Arts, and Social Change* (San Francisco: Jossey-Bass, 1995); Debra L. Holloway and Margaret D. LeCompte, "Becoming Somebody!: How Arts Programs Support Positive Identity for Middle School Girls," *Education and Urban Society* 33, no. 4 (August 2001): 388–408; Beth Krensky, "Going Beyond Zebra: A Middle School and Community-Based Arts Organization Collaborate for Change," *Education and Urban Society* 33, no. 4 (August 2001): 427–44.

22. Holloway and LeCompte, "Becoming Somebody!: How Arts Programs Support Positive Identity for Middle School Girls," 394.

23. Lev S. Vygotsky, *Thought and Language* (Cambridge, Mass.: The MIT Press, 1934/1962).

24. Lev S. Vygotsky, with Michael Cole, Vera John-Steiner, Sylvia Scribner, and Ellen Souberman, eds., *Mind in Society: The Development of Higher Psychological Processes* (Cambridge, Mass.: Harvard University Press, 1978), 86.

25. Barbara Rogoff, "Evaluating Development in the Process of Participation: Theory, Methods, and Practice Building on Each Other," draft chapter for *Change and Development: Issues of Theory, Application, and Method*, eds. E. Amsel and A. Renninger (Hillsdale, N.J.: Erlbaum, 1995), 2.

26. Barbara Rogoff, "Developing Understanding of the Idea of Communities of Learners," *Mind, Culture, and Activity* 1, no. 4 (1994): 222.

27. Rogoff, "Developing Understanding of the Idea of Communities of Learners," 222.

SECTION TWO

MODELING THE PRACTICE OF COMMUNITY ART

CHAPTER SIX

Murals, with Case Studies by Juliet Biagi

Mural, originating from the Latin word *murus*, means "wall." José Clemente Orozco, one of "Los Tres Grandes" ("The Three Great Ones") of the Mexican Mural Movement, believed that murals were the most generous form of painting. He said that a mural "cannot be turned into an object for personal profit; it cannot be hidden for the benefit of the privileged few. It is for the people. It is for everyone."[1] Indeed, because murals are often painted on surfaces accessible to the public, they are considered the people's art and are an ideal public art form. The following two case studies illustrate this accessible art form in a community and in a school. The chapter ends with a section on the essentials for an effective mural-making process and resources for creating murals.

Project YES Case Studies

About the Organization

Project YES, an acronym for Youth Envisioning Social change, creates leadership opportunities for young people through the arts and service learning. Project YES provides free programs in Lafayette, Colorado, that support young people in realizing their potential to create positive social change in their lives and communities. In 1991, Project YES began supporting youth in using the arts as a vehicle to make their voices heard about important social issues in their lives. Examples of youth-created art include a video about AIDS and teen pregnancy, graphic arts posters about recycling (displayed at the state capitol and in city bus shelters), and large posters calling for an end to handgun violence (displayed on the sides of public buses).

Project YES programs are youth centered, with young people making the critical decisions and taking on responsibility and ownership. In the Project YES workshop, young people build community within the group, identify community needs and assets, choose a social or environmental issue to address, create artwork that sends a message to the community about the issue, and present their artistic message through a public event. As a result of their participation, young people gain skills in critical thinking, community building, communication, conflict resolution, research, and a particular artistic medium.

A Community-Based Example: In Memory of Our Heroes

> "I like making art and helping people understand life and the things that happen to us."
>
> —"In Memory of our Heroes" mural participant, age 13

In 2001, Project YES youth created four traveling murals as part of a series titled *Youth Voices in the Community: Art and Community Youth Activism for the New Millennium*. The fourth and final mural, "In Memory of Our Heroes," was created in fall 2001 by a diverse group of eleven middle and high school students with the support of renowned local muralist Leo Tanguma. The three-dimensional mural, which addressed the September 11 terrorist attacks, was unveiled at the local fire station and later displayed at the local food bank, United Way office, and public library. In the youth's artist statement, they explain:

> "In Memory of Our Heroes" is a memorial. We decided on the name as a group to honor the people that died in the September 11 tragedy. This is a piece about unity, honor, peace, and heroes. What [is] painted are the towers on clouds, so it looks like they are in heaven. The people in the towers are the ones that could have been working at the time. On the bottom are the firefighters pulling people out of the rubble and helping them. The borders of the mural have many different flags from many different nations of the world. Inside the towers are different people with different occupations, backgrounds, and genders and of different ages, nationalities, and ethnicities. We feel passionate about this mural. It makes us feel good to express our emotions through art. We took it seriously. The Twin Towers are an important part of our history and we kids want to make a better future.

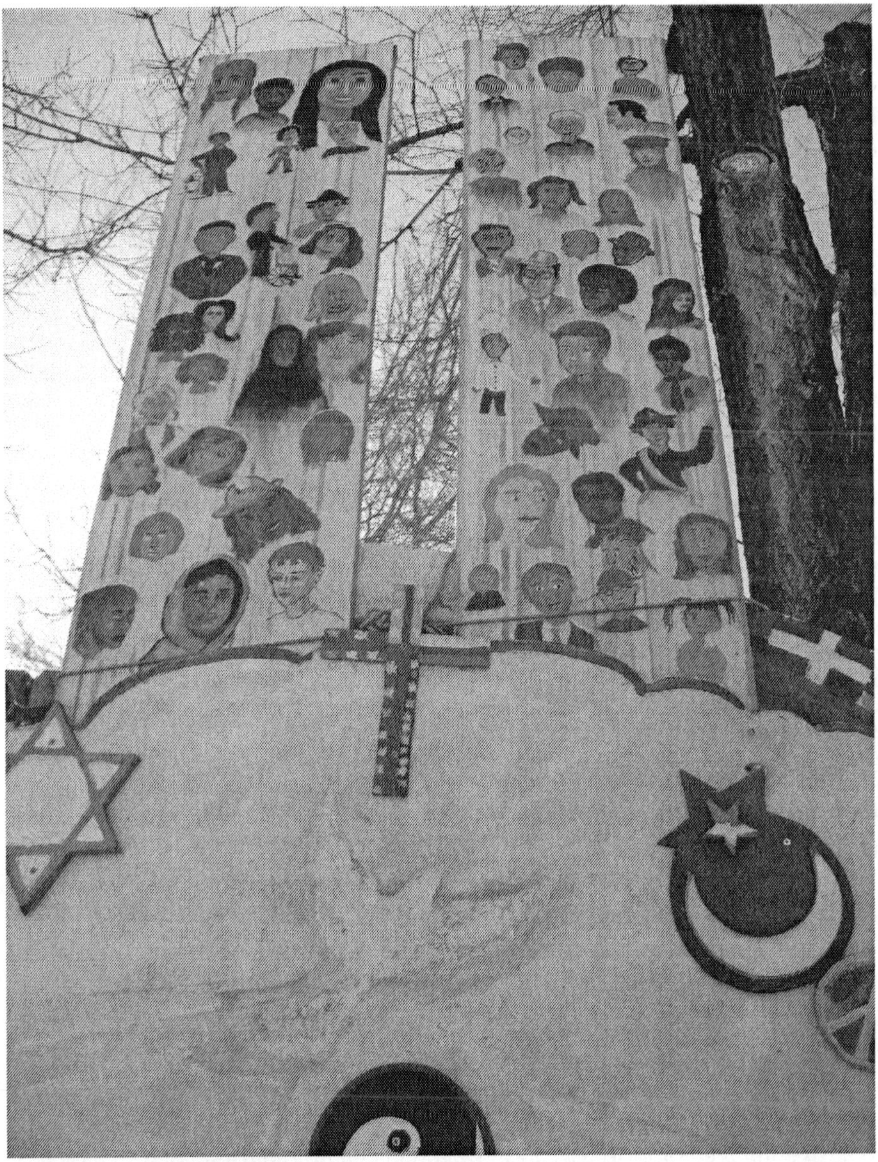

Figure 6.1. ***In Memory of Our Heroes,*** **three-dimensional mural, approximately 9' x 11', Project YES, Lafayette, Colorado, 2001.**

Photo credit: Jamie Rezmovits

Pre-Workshop Process

Project YES staff members created flyers and made school presentations to invite young people to create a public traveling mural with a well-known artist. Interested students completed project applications that asked about themselves, their interest in the project, and their past experience with leadership, the arts, and community projects.

Workshop Process

Introductions and community building: To inspire the participating youth to think about what they might create in their own communities, the collaborating artist shared slides of past youth-created art examples.

Issue exploration and selection: Soon after the introductions, the collaborating artist facilitated a discussion with the youth to identify various issues they felt were important in their lives and communities. The youth came to a consensus that the events of September 11 were currently most significant to them; therefore, they wanted to create their art about that topic. Together, the youth outlined their artistic concept, defining the piece as a tribute to those who had lost their lives. Additionally, the participating youth sought to display the diversity of the victims of September 11.

Mural design: Conceptualizing their end product, each young person sketched his or her vision for the mural, with many taking ideas of three-dimensionality from the slides the collaborating artist had shared with them. After reviewing each sketch, the youth agreed to base their design on one youth's rendition. They discussed the details of their design and how it would best convey their message to the community. The group then created a mini-model of their design.

Mural creation: The collaborating artist demonstrated color mixing, general painting procedures, and supplies maintenance. Based on the students' mini-model for their design, the collaborating artist determined the construction and assembly plan for the mural and used power tools to cut the students' designs from plywood. The youth and collaborating artist primed the plywood with white acrylic primer, built the structure for the mural, used charcoal to sketch the design on the plywood, and painted the twin towers, the giant cloud, the images of people, religious symbols, and flags using Liquitex acrylic paint.

Unveiling/celebration: Because the mural celebrated their "heroes," including firefighters who had risked and lost their lives on September 11, the participating youth unveiled their artwork at the local fire station. The unveiling attracted more than seventy-five community members, including members of Lafayette's volunteer fire department. Once the guests arrived, the youth unveiled their mural that had been draped with a large cloth. There were audible gasps as the crowd emotionally applauded the youth for their tribute. In addition to presenting their mural, the youth presented a slide show about the purpose and process of creating the mural and facilitated a question-and-answer session with a community discussion. Project YES staff recognized each young artist, as well as the collaborating artist, and invited guests to enjoy refreshments, look more closely at the artwork, and ask questions of individual youth.

Collaboration

For this workshop, Project YES partnered with Leo Tanguma, a renowned local Chicano muralist with commissioned work on display across the state of Colorado, throughout the United States, and in Germany. In addition to sharing his talent and insights with Project YES youth, the artist has supported groups of youth and adults in creating murals for social change for more than thirty years. Working with an artist of such caliber helped to attract youth to the project and provided them with an incredible artistic opportunity.

Project YES also partnered with four local organizations that chose to display the mural with the community at large during the six months following its creation and unveiling, thus supporting Project YES with the promotion of the youth's artistic message. In return, the partnering organizations received great compliments as the high-quality artwork graced their spaces for the duration of its display.

Five Essential Elements of this Project

1. Collaborating with a professional artist: Support from a knowledgeable artist helped to ensure the quality of the artistic product and develop the youth's artistic skills.
2. Creating a sense of community among the youth: Many of the youth involved in the mural project were engaged in games and activities at the Youth Center that developed trust within the mural group. These activities also encouraged leadership and community-building skills such as communication, conflict resolution, and teamwork.
3. Youths identifying an issue important to them: With a sense of community intact, the youth could safely share about issues that concerned them. The youth's choosing their topic for the mural was of utmost importance to the project's success.
4. Youths presenting their artistic message to the community: The opportunity to be seen in the community as leaders, to make their presentation alongside prominent adult leaders, and to be acknowledged for their ideas and their talent were critical components leading to the impact the project had on the youth.
5. Reflection: The youth were given the opportunity to reflect after the project's completion. By naming the skills they gained and talking about

their accomplishments, reflection helped reinforce and solidify the magnitude of their accomplishments, ensuring that learned skills and confidence were transferable to future endeavors.

Important Things to Remember

- Community youth art projects typically take longer than anticipated. Allocate extra time to ensure the quality of both the experience and the artistic product.
- Project success is dependent upon participants remaining involved throughout the project.
- Keep the size and assembly needs in mind when creating a traveling mural.

A School-Based Example: DIVERSITY

"I go out of my way so that I can drive by the DIVERSITY mural."

—Lafayette community member

In 2003, a high school student who had participated in a Project YES mural project asked the organization to collaborate with a group of students to create a mural about diversity at Centaurus High School in Lafayette, Colorado. The student wrote a letter to the high school principal and gained approval to paint over an outdated mural that had been created ten years earlier on a large cement retaining wall. Project YES held a twenty-week Art in the Community workshop in 2003, during which time seven students from Centaurus High School designed, built, and painted a three-dimensional mural, sixty-three feet wide by seven feet high, titled "DIVERSITY" for their school. Georgia Lindsay, a Project YES staff member as well as an artist and community activist, co-led the project with a former Project YES volunteer. The project received initial consulting support from a muralist and ongoing support from the school art teacher and two local carpenters.

The mural was painted in a prominent location visible from one of Lafayette's major streets, proudly representing the school and community's value of diversity. The youth's artistic treatment of the theme came through in two ways. First, the youth painted a giant sun and moon on either end, with a tree growing in the middle. The youth explained, "The sun and moon together represent opposites . . . the tree bridges the differences, so that through the tree, the sun can see the moon and the moon can see the sun. The clouds and the sun rays go through and around the tree to help represent that visually." In addition to the painted images, the mural has a three-dimensional aspect, with large wooden letters spelling D-I-V-E-R-S-I-T-Y mounted on the

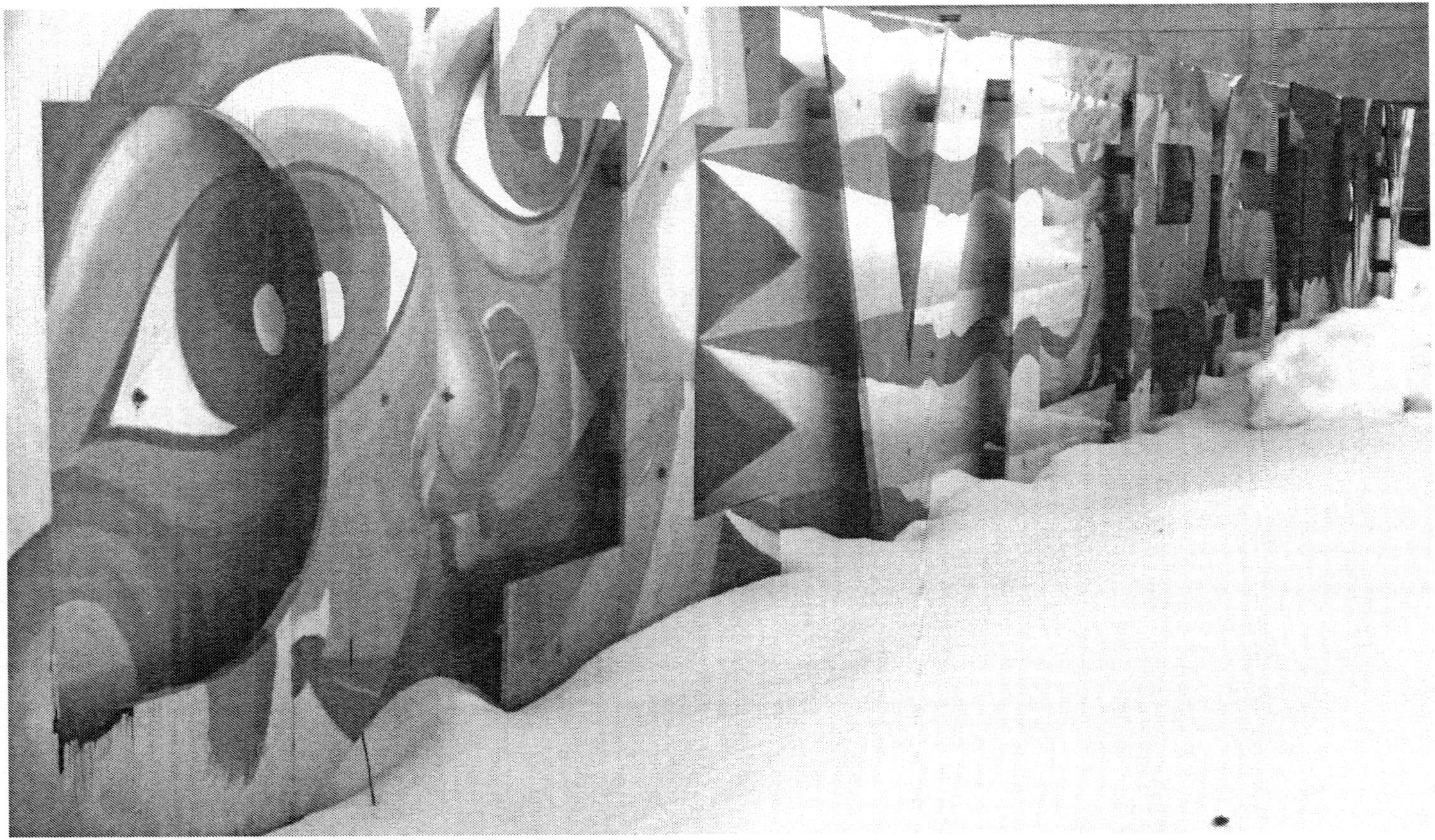

Figure 6.2. ***DIVERSITY***, **three-dimensional mural, 63' x 7', Project YES, Lafayette, Colorado, 2003.**
Photo credit: Jamie Rezmovits

front of the mural. The letters are painted to look like the background so that the word is visible but subtle.

Pre-Workshop Process

Due to the project's collaborative nature, Project YES held several meetings that included the school principal, the art teacher, and Project YES staff to share expectations and ensure a smooth process. The workshop co-leaders created a flyer for the school, urging students to "Be a Legend" by helping create a monumental piece of art for their school. Co-leaders also made presentations in classes and with school clubs, asking interested youth to fill out applications.

Workshop Process

Introductions and community building: The youth participated in games and activities to get to know one another. They shared about themselves, explored group dynamics, talked about what they brought to the group, and examined their individual and collective hopes for the project.

Issue exploration and selection: The youth talked about what diversity meant to them and explored different aspects of diversity in their school and community. They also researched aspects of diversity through student and teacher surveys on issues of cultural diversity, stereotyping, and discrimination.

Mural design: Each youth participant created his or her own sketch about diversity and presented it to the group, along with its intended meaning. After examining each illustration and corresponding message, the group elected one member of the group to sketch the collective visions. The group then conceived its artistic concept, with the sun and moon as opposites helping the tree to grow and the three-dimensional letters spelling out the word DIVERSITY.

Mural creation: Creating a 441-square-foot mural outdoors was not easy! Two carpenters and a consulting artist supported the youth in building and priming panels measuring nine feet wide by seven feet high, cutting the large letters, and attaching the panels and letters to the cement retaining wall. The youth sketched their design onto the wood panels (made from half-inch plywood and primed with white latex house paint) and letters (made from one-inch plywood and primed with house paint) and then painted the images. They then glued and screwed the plywood panels onto frames made from two-by-two- and two-by-four-inch lumber (depending on what was available) that were primed with white latex house paint. At that point, the youth attached the plywood panels to the concrete wall with half-inch concrete anchor bolts and construction glue. First, the group drilled holes in the concrete and matching holes in the panels. Then they pounded the anchor bolts (about ten anchor bolts for every seven-foot by twelve-foot panel) into the concrete, put construction glue on the frame of the panels, and hung them on the extended anchor bolts. Finally, they put rust-resistant washers and nuts on the outside of the bolts and painted over them. The entire process took more than 420 human hours, but the committed youth saw the project through as it extended from the spring into the middle of summer.

Unveiling/celebration: The youth planned and implemented their unveiling event and presented their mural to more than fifty family members, teachers, administrators, students, and community members on a summer afternoon. They designed invitations, prepared food, created programs, and wrote individual speeches explaining their process and artistic message.

Collaboration

The partnership with the high school was mutually beneficial, as Project YES had the opportunity to work with the school's students while receiving great exposure in the community through the high-profile project. Additionally, the school's senior class made a generous financial contribution to help make the project possible, along with the support given through the local United Way. In return, the school received both a phenomenal, professional-quality piece of public art adorning the campus entrance and an opportunity for its students to gain leadership skills while engaging in a unique art project.

The school's art teacher was a key player in the process, recruiting students for the project, acting as the sponsoring faculty member, offering technical support throughout the process, and recruiting his brother to contribute his carpentry skills. The experience afforded the teacher an opportunity to experience Project YES's youth-centered model of arts education and to work with his students in a different context outside the classroom setting.

Four Essential Elements of the Project

1. Structure: The process of community building, issue exploration, art design, and creation, along with a public unveiling and celebration, served as the foundation for the project's success.
2. Youth–adult partnerships, youth decision making, and power sharing: Youth and adults worked side by side, with the adults sharing power and empowering the youth to make major decisions.
3. Unveiling to the community: Often, youth fully realize the profound nature of their accomplishment only after the presentation to the community and the awe-struck response and positive feedback from others.

The public presentation also serves to augment the artistic message, allowing the community to hear the message directly from the youth instead of relying solely on the art to speak for itself. The community unveiling often alters the way the community views the young people and, in turn, the way the youth view themselves.

4. Reflection: Reflection is a critical component before, during, and after the workshop. The co-leaders and youth are consistently planning, acting, and reflecting on their work For example, discussing questions like "Why are we doing this?" "What's working?" and "What can be done to make things better?" help to guide and strengthen the process, celebrating growth and successes along the way.

Important Things to Remember

- A workshop of this nature is most effective when youth identify the topic for their artwork. Even though the topic of diversity was generated by a young person earlier in the year, the topic needs to be owned by the entire group of participating youth in a collaborative art-making process.
- Using the artistic medium during the community-building phase of the workshop is critical. Whenever possible, find ways to incorporate the art form into the games and activities designed to build community and explore social issues. This helps support mastery of the medium.
- When a piece of art is representing a school, the issue and its treatment are no longer solely up to the youth. A school principal or school board may need to approve sketches before an art project is officially started at the school. In a youth-centered project, the project's parameters must be defined with the youth at the beginning so that they are an understood part of the process and not perceived as a loss of power or decision-making ability.

The following section provides a brief overview of the essential components for an effective mural process.

Essentials for the Mural Process

Please refer to chapter 2 for an overview of the community-art process that we suggest as a framework. If you are planning a community-based mural, we strongly recommend collaborating with a professional mural artist and using the recommended resources to gain an in-depth understanding of the mural-making process. Below are the essential components we suggest for making a mural.

Golden Spike

2005

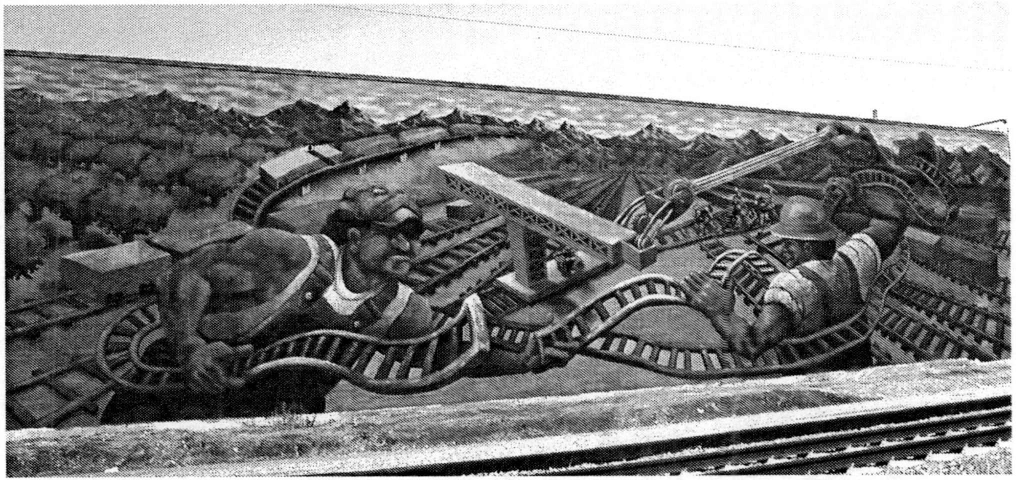

Figure 6.3. ***Golden Spike*** **outdoor mural, 25' x 100', V. Kim Martinez and students from her mural arts class at the University of Utah, Salt Lake City, Utah, 2005.**

Photo credit: V. Kim Martinez

Choosing/Securing a Wall

- Choose a surface that can be seen from a distance, is free of obstructions, and is relatively smooth.
- Ensure that you have obtained written legal permission to use the wall from the property owner.

Designing the Mural

- Consider how the mural is viewed and design it accordingly. Adjust the image when it is predominantly viewed from one side.[2]
- Think about the exterior and interior spaces. Incorporate the existing building configuration into the composition.
- Consider these questions when deciding on the final design:
  - Is it accessible to all?
  - Is the imagery legible and immediate?
  - Does the image address political, historical, cultural, and contextual ideas and activities?
- Prepare a final scale model of the mural before painting it on a permanent surface.

Painting the Mural

- Prepare the surface by removing paint and residue and thoroughly cleaning it.[3]
- Transfer the design to the wall using the grid or projection method.
- Decide whether to paint using one or multiple layers. Underpainting, which can either contrast or harmonize with the top layers of paint, is an optional step; however, it is strongly recommended if you are painting outside on a white surface, because it lessens the sun's glare.
- Paint the mural on a wall or parachute cloth[4] surface. If painting outside, ensure that participants wear sunglasses. The glare of the sun reflecting off a wall can damage participants' eyes.
- Coat the finished mural to protect it from elements, pollutants, and vandalism and to prevent fading over time.[5]

Avoiding Risks

- Spend the time and resources needed to ensure that a good wall is selected and prepared and that the best materials are used. Too often, hundreds of hours are spent designing and painting a mural that lasts only a short time because the paint fades, the wall seeps chemicals or rust onto the mural, or the wall crumbles away.[6]

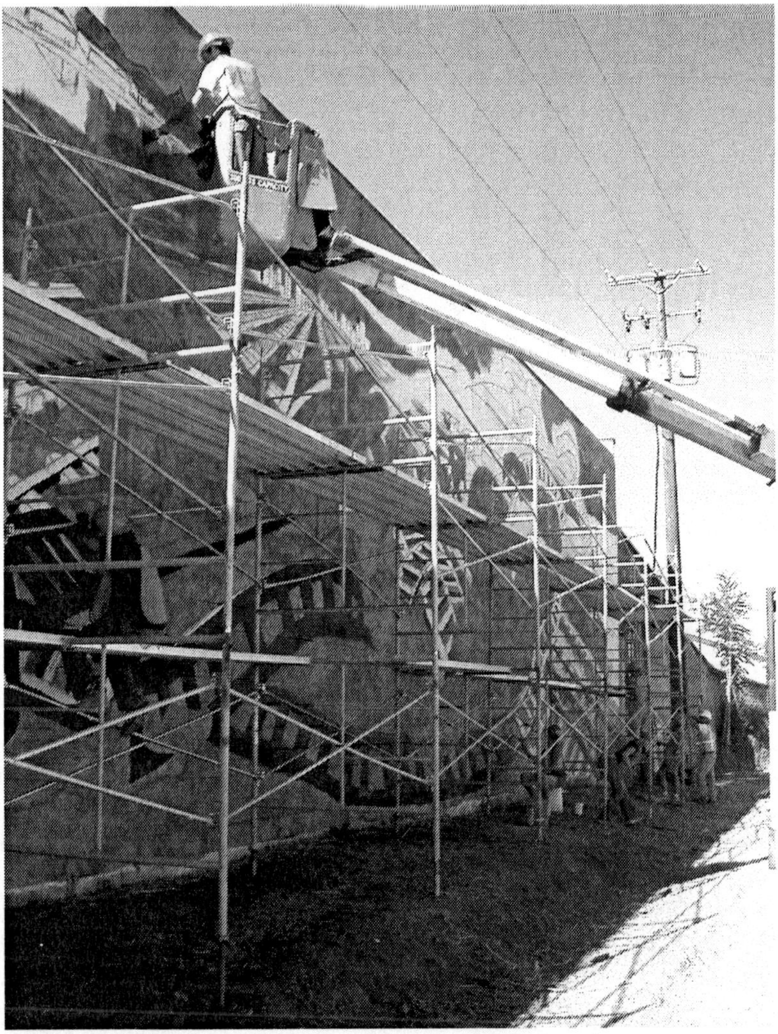

Figure 6.4. ***Golden Spike*, underpainting, 25' x 100', V. Kim Martinez and students from her mural arts class at the University of Utah, Salt Lake City, Utah, 2005.**

Photo credit: V. Kim Martinez

- Consider the necessary amount of time and number of participants when selecting the level of collaboration for a mural process. Underestimating the amount of time needed for design and execution is common.

Please refer to the following print and web-based resources for more information about the history and process of creating murals.

Mural Resources

Case Study Contact Information

Project YES
200 E. South Boulder Rd. Ste C2, Lafayette, CO 80026
(303) 926-0306
www.project-yes.org

Print Resources

Ancona, George. *Murals: Walls That Sing*. New York: Marshall Cavendish Corp., 2003.

Bank Downs, Linda. *Diego Rivera: The Detroit Industry Murals*. New York: W.W. Norton & Company, 1999.

Barnett, Alan. *Community Murals: The People's Art*. New York: Cornwall Books, 1984.

Braun-Reinitz, Janet, and Rochelle Shicoff. *The Mural Book: A Practical Guide for Educators*. Aspen, Colo., and Glenview, Ill.: Crystal Productions Co., 2001.

Cockroft, Eva, and Holly Barnet-Sánchez. *Signs From the Heart: California Chicano Murals*. Los Angeles: SPARC, 1990.

Cockroft, Eva, John Weber, and James Cockroft. *Toward A People's Art: The Contemporary Mural Movement*. New York: E. P. Dalton & Co., Inc., 1998/1977.

Drescher, Timothy. *San Francisco Murals: Community Creates Its Muse 1914–1994*. St. Paul, Minn.: Pogo Press, 1994.

Golden, Jane, Robin Rice, David Graham, Jack Ramsdale, and Natalie Pompilio. *More Philadelphia Murals and the Stories They Tell*. Philadelphia: Temple University Press, 2006.

Golden, Jane, Robin Rice, and Monica Yant Kinney. *Philadelphia Murals and the Stories They Tell*. Philadelphia: Temple University Press, 2002.

Gude, Olivia, and Jeff Huebner. *Urban Art Chicago: A Guide to Community Murals, Mosaics, and Sculpture*. Chicago: Ivan R. Dee, Inc., 2000.

Prigoff, James, and Robin Dunitz. *Walls of Heritage, Walls of Pride: African American Murals*. Petaluma, Calif.: Pomegranate Communications, Inc., 2000.

Rochfort, Desmond. *Mexican Muralists: Orozco, Rivera, Siqueiros*. Great Britain: Laurence King Publishing, 1993.

Web Resources

Chicago Public Art Group—www.cpag.net
Golden Artist Colors—www.goldenpaints.com
Liquitex Paints—www.liquitex.com
Philadelphia Mural Arts Program—www.muralarts.org
Social and Public Art Resource Center (SPARC)—www.sparcmurals.org

Notes

1. George Ancona, *Murals: Walls That Sing* (New York: Marshall Cavendish Corp., 2003), 3.

2. Valerie Kim Martinez, a professor at the University of Utah, teaches a comprehensive mural class that educates students about the fundamental elements of mural making and provides them with the opportunity to design and paint large-scale community murals. To this end, she teaches her students about the techniques as well as the social, political, and historical implications of the medium. Portions of "Designing the Model" are drawn from Valerie Kim Martinez, *Working Draft: Mural Design and Technique* (Salt Lake City: University of Utah, 2006).

3. See Jane Golden, Robin Rice, and Monica Yant Kinney, *Philadelphia Murals and the Stories They Tell* (Philadelphia: Temple University Press, 2002), 15–16, and the Chicago Public Art Group website (www.cpag.net) for detailed information about preparing the mural surface.

4. Murals may be painted onto panels of parachute cloth (officially known as polytab non-woven), a thin, felt-like material that looks like dryer sheets. Muralist Sarah Moyer suggests that it is easier to achieve greater detail with parachute cloth than painting directly on a wall. This is due to the fact that walls generally have a rougher texture than the smooth cloth, and the cloth enables artists to transfer a mural design more accurately. With parachute cloth, painters can paint in a sheltered indoor space. If this type of cloth is used, it should be adhered to the mural wall with acrylic gel, which is done by "buttering" both surfaces—the wall and the cloth—with acrylic gel medium. Parachute cloth may be ordered from QST Industries. It is called polytab 20R and costs approximately $200 for 250 yards.

5. There are clear acrylic coatings as well as clear ultraviolet protection coatings that may be used to prevent the mural's fading over time. Additionally, a graffiti coating can be painted over the surface of a completed mural that can be cleaned without damaging the mural. For instance, a product called Soluvar from Liquitex protects murals from pollutants and graffiti.

6. "Avoiding Risks" is informed by muralist Sarah Moyer.

CHAPTER SEVEN

Photography, with Case Study by Jennifer Atkinson

The word *photography* is derived from the Greek words *phot* (light) and *graphos* (writing). Photography literally means "writing with light." The variety and accessibility of cameras, as well as different printing and projecting options, make photography a highly effective community-art form. Large groups of participants can shoot images that may be collectively displayed in multiple places, including books, exhibitions, banners, or the sides of buildings. The following case study illustrates how a community-art photography project culminated in the publication of the book *A Piece of Peace: Kids Share Their Lives Through Poetry, Art & Photography*. The chapter ends with a section on the essentials for effectively creating photography projects followed by resources for the photography process.

A Piece of Peace Case Study

About the Organization

The Boys & Girls Clubs of Boston, Charlestown Club, one of nine clubs that make up Boys & Girls Clubs of Boston, is a youth-development organization for six- to eighteen-year-olds. Serving the children and teens of the Charlestown, Massachusetts, community since 1893, the Charlestown Club offers a wide variety of drop-in activities and scheduled classes organized by core program, such as arts, education, life skills, sports, technology, fitness and recreation, leadership, and character development. The Charlestown Club is staffed by more than fifteen full-time employees, fifteen part-time

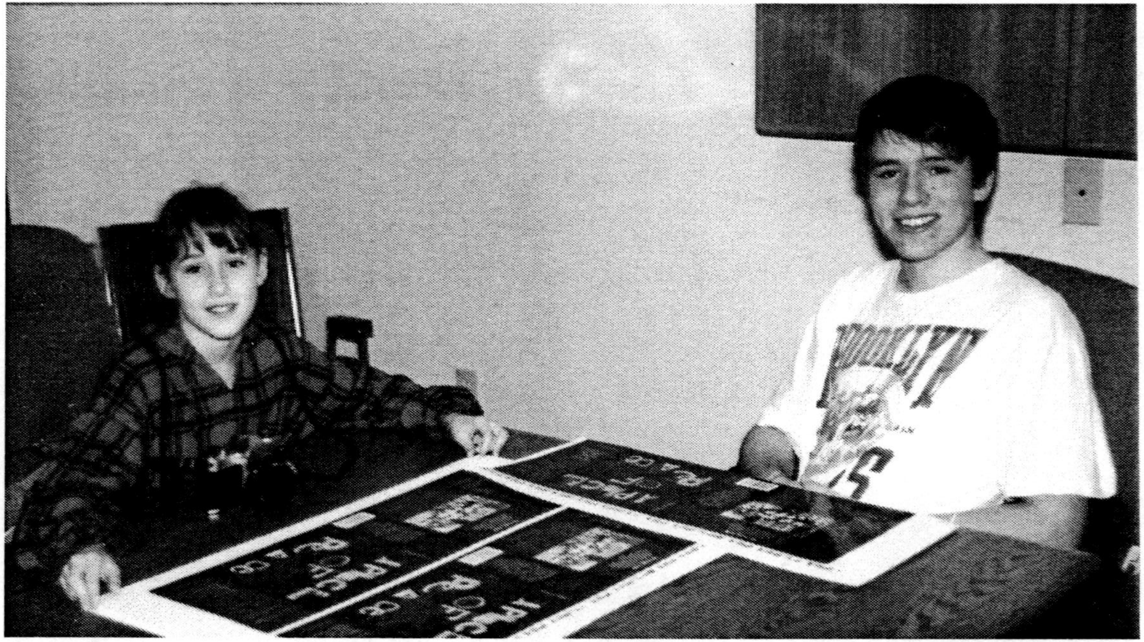

Figure 7.1. *Piece of Peace* book project, Boys & Girls Clubs of Boston, Charlestown Club, Charlestown, Massachusetts, 1994.

employees, and ten junior employees and serves daily about 225 of its 700 members. Staff members develop long-standing relationships with club members, encouraging them to take risks in a safe setting, set attainable goals for themselves, and have fun. The Charlestown Club is a place where young people can find a way to feel they belong and are a part of something that is bigger than themselves.

A Community-Based Example: A Piece of Peace Book Project

A *Piece of Peace* began as a discussion-based class about peace that involved creating art in several media and culminated in a book that included writing, painting, drawing, printmaking, and photography by Club members. Staff members in the art department—Beth Krensky, Jenny Atkinson, and Eliza Hemenway—had talked for a number of years about how young people needed to be able to express their feelings of fear and hope about the issues they faced in their lives, their communities, and the world. They believed that the arts were a safe venue for this kind of expression. Club members met weekly in two age groups, six- to eight-year-olds and nine- to twelve-year-olds. In the initial classes, members set ground rules and discussed the importance of respecting everyone's experiences.[1] During subsequent sessions, they read accounts of people and communities that were working toward peace despite many obstacles, studied the work of famous artists as well as other young people, and learned the techniques needed for each art form. They also learned more about the history of Charlestown, their Boston neighborhood. Then they turned to their own experiences and began expressing their emotions about events in their lives and their dreams for the future.

Art Making

Much of the artwork was initially simplistic, but as the club members worked together, critiquing their work and building a level of trust with themselves and others in their groups, the work became more personal and powerful. Through the process of creating more and more artwork, the young people started to believe that they would create a book. In one of the sessions, an eleven-year-old club member suggested the name "A Piece of Peace," and the others agreed immediately that this title encompassed the work they were trying to do. The youth participated in three eight-week-long clinics for each of the art media: photography, poetry, and painting/drawing/printmaking. Skilled artists who had training and experience with young people *and* the arts led the art workshops. Young people used real materials: they wrote in journals, took photos with 35-mm cameras, developed

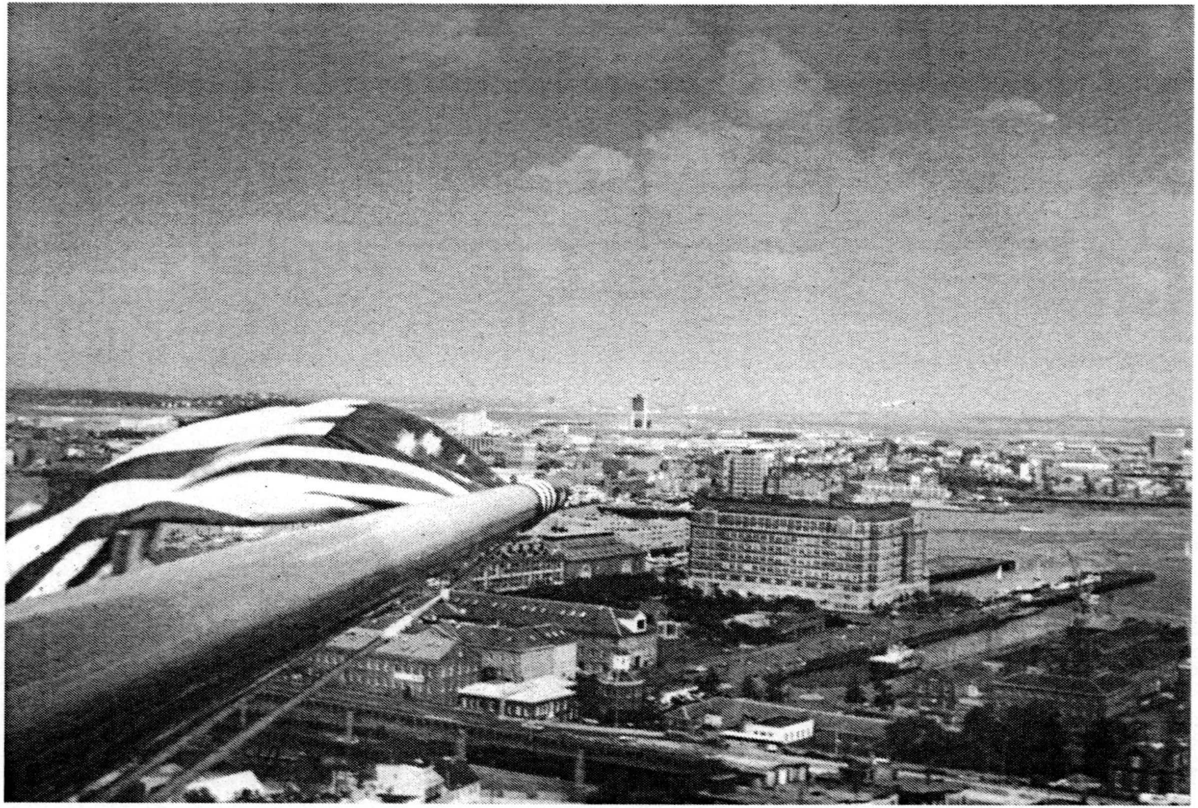

Figure 7.2. ***Home Sweet Home***, black-and-white photograph, Patrick Gould, age 13, ***A Piece of Peace*** book project, Boys & Girls Clubs of Boston, Charlestown Club, Charlestown, Massachusetts, 1995.

photos in a darkroom, and used professional art supplies for painting and drawing classes.

During the photography sessions, the youth used two kinds of cameras: Pentax K-1000 SLR cameras and point-and-shoot cameras. Although the participants were able to use point-and-shoot cameras some of the time, everyone learned how to operate the manual SLR cameras, even the six-year-olds. The photography workshop covered such topics as how to operate the camera (focus, depth of field, adjusting the aperture), how to compose an image (angle, light and shadow, depth of field, distance from the object), how to experiment with subject matter and composition, how to develop and print photographs, and how to critique and choose from multiple images.

In addition to the eight-week workshops, many club members participated in other photography classes held at the Charlestown Club. The club had a full black-and-white process darkroom where members could learn to process film and print photographs. Some of the older participants became darkroom assistants, helping younger members learn the basics of photography and assisting the instructor by developing and printing photographs for the project. The members also took field trips throughout Charlestown and the greater Boston area, taking pictures that represented peace or the lack of peace in their lives.

Although the workshops lasted only eight weeks for each medium, members wrote throughout the program, and participants continued to use the different artistic media as a way to express themselves throughout the peace classes. For example, they were each given journals that they kept with them, writing whenever they were inspired. At each session, members could share from their journals if they wanted to. Older members served as "human typewriters" for younger participants who could not yet write, recording their thoughts for them. Another writing project included conducting oral histories of town residents. This activity allowed young people to learn about peace or the lack of peace through the eyes of others in the community, especially the town elders, and it helped members develop listening and interviewing skills.

Publication

The art practitioners who facilitated the community-art project believed that young people's ideas and visions were not heard or taken seriously and felt that youth had important things to say that should be heard. In searching for a publisher that would allow club members to be a part of the decision-making

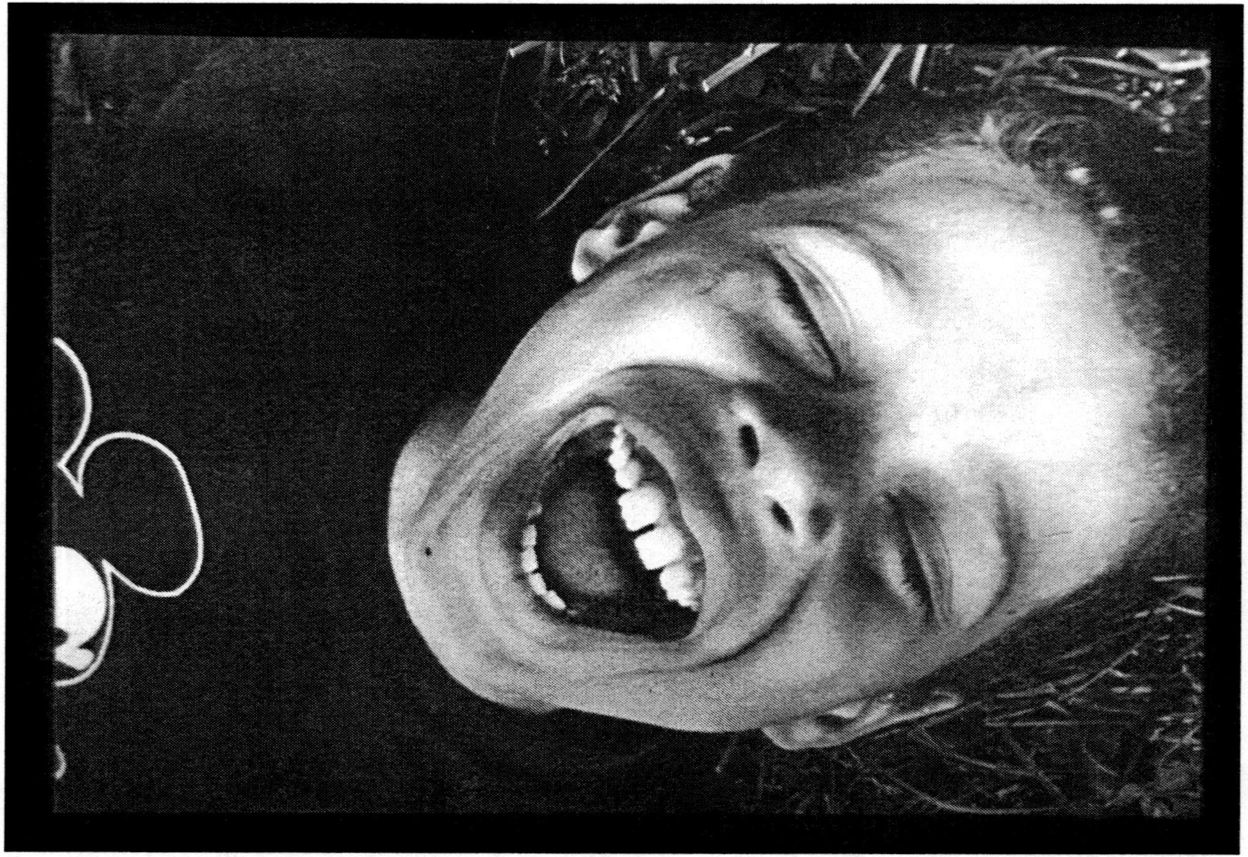

Figure 7.3. *Reggie*, black-and-white photograph, Caitlin Gossett, age 11, *A Piece of Peace* book project, Boys & Girls Clubs of Boston, Charlestown Club, Charlestown, Massachusetts, 1995.

process during publication, staff members decided to work with Font & Center Press in Weston, Massachusetts. Four of the almost-sixty club members who had participated in classes were selected as youth editors, and they spent several weeks combing through the classes' poetry and artwork and making decisions about what to include in the final book. They also discussed how the artwork should appear in the book and made decisions about the front and back cover design. In addition, they created a list of likely advocates and wrote to them requesting support for the book. The back cover of *A Piece of Peace* provides responses from some of these advocates, including Howard Zinn, Deborah Prothrow-Stith, Bob Guillemin (Sidewalk Sam), Nancy Carlsson-Paige, and Abelardo Morell.

Publicity

The four youth editors also were a part of creating the publicity plan. They created and reviewed press releases and participated in almost all the press events, including television and radio interviews, book signings at local bookstores, and discussions at the public library. They talked about the process of creating the artwork as well as creating the book. Here they describe their goals for the project and how the project changed them:

> *A Piece of Peace* was created by fifty-seven kids whose ages ranged from six to fourteen years old. The young people come from many racial backgrounds. The Piece of Peacers are living in Charlestown, a very historic neighborhood just a mile from downtown Boston. Some of the Piece of Peacers live in the Bunker Hill project and others live in houses or apartments. . . . They did this project to express themselves through writing or art, to inspire people or just to have fun. We, the editors, know that everyone doesn't want to make peace. We know this book might not change the world. We hope that you, as the reader, will keep reading the book over and over again and think about what your piece of making peace can be.
>
> —Youth Editors' Statement

Celebration

When the book was published, the young people who participated in the project, as well as community members, the press, participants' families, and others, attended a book-signing celebration. The young people were thrilled to celebrate their success and sign copies of the books. One eight-year-old, after signing a few books, started shaking his hand and said, "If I have to sign too many more books, my hand is going to be sore!" This celebration brought closure to the event and also allowed many of the young people to feel that their work had been recognized. For participants who were not involved in the ensuing promotion of the book, this event was especially important. Font & Center Press provided free copies of the book for each of the sixty young people who participated in the project.

Reflection

Young people changed during this project. Members who were afraid to talk about the violence they saw around them slowly opened up and expressed their fears. Others learned about the importance of supporting their friends through listening, constructive criticism, and encouragement. All participants learned more about personal power when they saw a book to which they had contributed for sale in a bookstore. More than one made a comment like "If I can make a book, I can do anything!"

In creating and implementing such a project as *A Piece of Peace*, creating a setting in which young people feel safe is critical. Since these topics are often not frequently discussed, it may also take time for young people (and adults) to have a comfort level (and even a vocabulary) for expression. In addition, expression through the arts can provide a means of expression for people who do not have the words to describe what they want to communicate to their audience.

Promoting the work of the young people was important in this project. The staff and young people talked from the beginning about the importance of having the artwork seen and heard by a wider audience. Although there were some promotional opportunities while the young people were creating work, most of the promotion occurred once the book was published. At that point it was easier for the young people to respond to people's questions. On many occasions, adults wanted to speak for the young people, and the staff leaders often had to explain to others that the youth needed to speak for themselves. Making this clear to adults from the outset was important because it was not common practice.

Essential Elements of the Project

- Setting ground rules and expecting everyone to respect each other are critical if young people are going to be able to talk about and create artwork about sensitive topics.
- Studying the work of others who have addressed these issues will help the group and each participant to build a language to talk about the issues.
- Including experts in the various art media and treating participants as experts increase the artistic integrity of the final product.

- Giving participants time as a group and on their own to reflect on the work that they have done enables them to recognize their capacities.
- Allowing young people to represent themselves empowers them.

The following section provides a brief overview of the essential components for an effective photographic process.

Essentials for the Photographic Process

Please refer to chapter 2 for an overview of the community-art process that we suggest as a framework. If you are planning a community-based photography project, we strongly recommend collaborating with a professional photographer and using the recommended resources to gain an in-depth understanding of the photographic process.

Following are the essential components we suggest for the photographic process.[2]

While the most basic information may not apply to all groups, the following skills can be applied to an authentic, meaningful project in order for the participants to develop the techniques and vocabulary necessary for competency in composition.

Learning How to Take Photographs

- Have participants understand and practice the concepts of *angle*, *pan*, *distance*, *level*, *focus*, *framing*, *light*, and the *rule of thirds*. Participants can learn by taking photographs as well as by viewing and critiquing photographic images that illustrate the concepts. Viewing photographs by important photographers from different historical periods, as well as from different cultural perspectives, provides participants with an inclusive overview of the medium. In addition, viewing images from the same geographic area as the project's location connects participants with their unique locale. If the project includes youth, using youth-created photographs makes the project more authentic.[3]
  - *Angle* is the angle or tilt at which one holds the camera while shooting a photograph. Concepts should include *up angle*, *down angle*, or *straight*. Participants may take three shots of one image using each of the different angles. It is helpful if the participants physically engage in the activity. For instance, they may lie on the ground to shoot an *up angle* or climb up high to shoot a *down angle*.
  - *Pan* refers to the different places from which one can take a photograph. The photographer may stand in front of the subject (forward) or on either side.

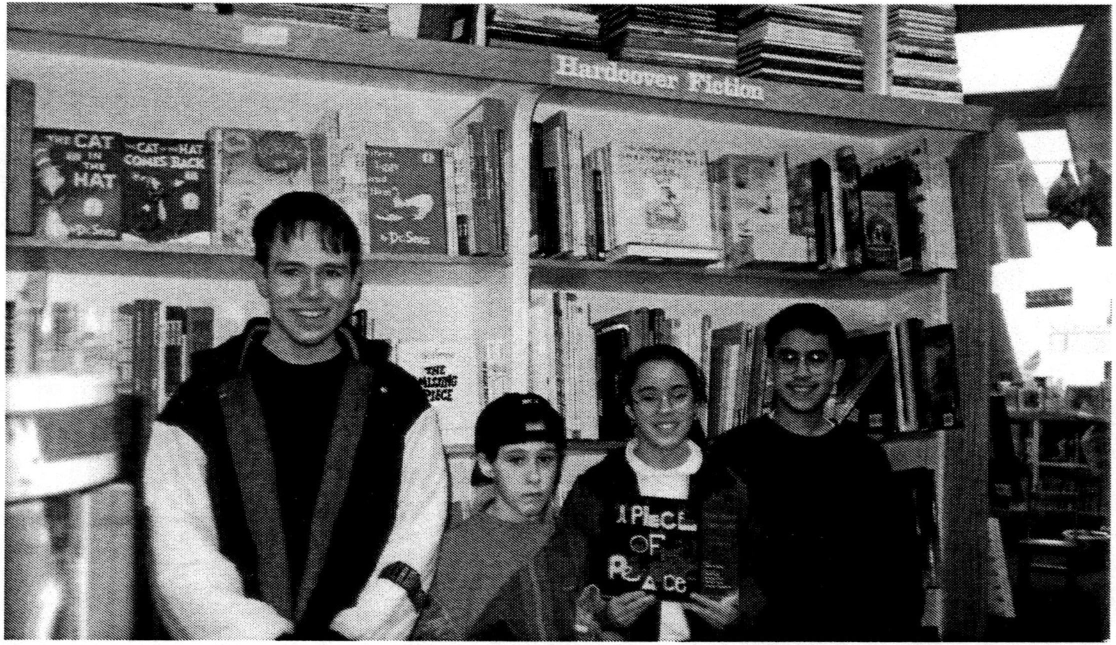

Figure 7.4. *Piece of Peace* project, Boys & Girls Clubs of Boston, Charlestown Club, Charlestown, Massachusetts, 1994.

  - Gradations of *distance* include very close, close, middle, far, and very far. Participants may practice shooting at different distances through special activities, and after some level of mastery has been achieved, the zoom function may be discussed and practiced.
  - *Level* refers to the height—eye level, high, or low—from which the photographer shoots the subject. Level differs from *angle* because angle refers to the camera's tilt rather than the height from which the photograph is shot.
  - *Focus* may be on a continuum from sharp to soft and changes, depending on distance, angle, and depth of field. *Depth of field* refers to the area in a photograph that is in focus. It depends on the length of the lens, how much the lens is open (the *f-stop*), and the distance that exists between the camera and the subject being photographed. The less the lens is open (the larger the f-stop), the greater the depth of field will be.
  - *Framing* is what the photographer includes in the photograph—what is placed within its four edges. When framing a photograph, participants should consider horizontal versus vertical orientation of the subject.
  - The photographer should also consider the quality of *light*. Natural light, indoor light, and flash create different types of lighting that change how the colors and subjects look; the direction of light onto the subject is another important factor.
  - The *rule of thirds* is a technique used to divide the frame of a photograph into thirds—both horizontally and vertically—which breaks the picture plane into an imaginary tic-tac-toe board. Placement of the subject onto the intersection of two lines may improve the composition.

Processing, Editing, and Printing the Film

- Photographs may be *processed* in a darkroom set up specifically for the community-art project,[4] or they may be taken to a professional photo lab to be processed. Local photo labs often provide education discounts or may even develop the prints at no cost.
- Photographs may be *edited* in the darkroom or, if they are digital prints, on a computer using photo-editing software.[5] (Digital cameras often come with editing software.) These applications provide basic editing, such as cropping and adding text to the photograph.
- The type of photo paper or substrate is an important consideration when *printing* photographs.[6] Images may also be printed on such surfaces as metal, watercolor paper, fabrics, mylar, or vinyl. Several relatively simple techniques are available for creating prints, such as photo transfers and photograms.

- A *photo transfer* is a method of transferring an image onto paper or another surface. Photos can be transferred to fabric by printing or copying an image onto photo transfer paper. This paper is made for inkjet and laser printers as well as copy machines. Once the image has been printed or copied onto the photo transfer paper, it can be ironed onto a fabric surface.
- Another photo transfer technique involves making a color or black-and-white copy of a photograph and transferring it onto a surface like paper, wood, fabric, or metal with acrylic gel medium. The multistep process begins by painting three layers of acrylic gel medium onto the receiving surface of the transferred image, alternating the brush strokes on the painted layers such that one layer is entirely vertical and the next layer is entirely horizontal. It is important to allow the gel medium to dry between coats. Once the three layers have been applied and the surface is dry, liberally brush with acrylic gel medium the front surface of the image to be transferred. While the gel medium is still wet, place the photograph face down onto the surface of the dried acrylic gel medium and rub the back of the photograph. The ink will transfer into the acrylic gel medium. (Because the transfer creates a mirror image, any text should be placed on the image "backwards" using photo-editing software.) To remove the photograph paper, two techniques are available: either wait until the gel medium is *almost* dry and then slowly peel the paper off, or wait until the gel medium has completely dried (at least twelve hours) and then gently rub the paper off with a wet paper towel or cloth. (Because the latter option is less prone to mistakes, it may be more appropriate when working with youth.)
- *Photograms* are contact prints, created by placing opaque or translucent objects onto light-sensitive paper and exposing it to light. The objects block the light and create a picture or pattern on the paper. Photograms may be created in the darkroom or in sunlight. To create a photogram, first place objects on the paper, expose to sunlight or light from an enlarger (use standard exposure times for specific types of paper), and process the paper according to the manufacturer's instructions for the paper. Photograms may be made using photo paper (if using a darkroom) or cyanotype paper (if using sunlight). Cyanotype paper can be made or purchased as "sun print" paper from any art supply or art education supply catalog or store. We recommend purchasing the paper so that no contact with chemicals is necessary for production or processing.

- Photographs may be drawn and painted on, cut apart, used in a collage, or included in a two-dimensional or sculptural work. Text may also be used as part of the final artwork.[7]

Avoiding Risks

- Ensure that the participants receive the training and practice necessary to produce high-quality work. Too often, community-based photography projects rely on one-time photo shoots that produce work without the depth found in longer-term projects where participants have learned technical and artistic skills.
- If using digital cameras, shoot in high resolution so the images may be enlarged and still look sharp.
- Require participants to obtain written permission from the people they want to photograph so that future legal display issues are prevented.

Please refer to the following print and web-based resources for more information about the history and process of photography.

Photography Resources

Case Study Contact Information

Boys & Girls Clubs of Boston, Charlestown Clubhouse
15 Green Street
Charlestown, MA 02129
(617) 242-1775
www.bgcb.org

Print Resources

Blacklow, Laura. *New Dimensions in Photo Processes: A Step By Step Manual, Third Edition*. Burlington, Mass.: Focal Press, 2000.

Ewald, Wendy, and Alexandra Lightfoot. *I Wanna Take Me a Picture: Teaching Photography and Writing to Children*. Durham, N.C.: Center for Documentary Studies, 2001.

Franklin, Kristine, and Nancy McGirr. eds. *Out of the Dump: Writings and Photographs by Children from Guatemala*. New York: Lothrop, Lee and Shepard Books, 1995.

Freed, Les, and Sumi Das. *Tech TV's Digital Camera and Imaging Guide*. Indianapolis: QUE, 2002.

Haslam, Andrew. *Make it Work!: Photography*. Princeton, N.J.: Two-Can Publishing, 2000.

Hubbard, Jim. *Shooting Back: A Photographic View of Life by Homeless Children*. San Francisco: Chronicle Books, 1991.

Hubbard, Jim. *Shooting Back from the Reservation: A Photographic View of Life by Native American Children*. New York: New Press, 1994.

Johnson, Neil. *National Geographic Photography Guide for Kids*. Washington, D.C.: National Geographic Society, 2001.

Krensky, Beth, with Neale Boyle, Roselyn Boyle, Patrick Gould, and Caitlin Rodriguez. *A Piece of Peace: Kids Share Their Lives through Poetry, Art & Photography*. Newton, Mass.: Font & Center Press, 1995. (Available from www.project-yes.org.)

London, Barbara, and John Upton. *Photography, 6th Edition*. Reading, Mass.: Addison-Wesley, 1997.

Web Resources

Center for Creative Photography—www.creativephotography.org

The Center for Creative Photography provides free online educators' guides for teaching photography to youth.

Children as Photographers—www.cap.ac.uk

The Children as Photographers website includes a free "Children as Photographers: Education Resource Pack," designed for teachers and concentrating on the art and design curriculum. The packet contains twelve photographs taken by youth as well as suggestions for activities to be used in conjunction with the images.

FOTOFEST, Inc.—www.fotofest.org

FOTOFEST is an international nonprofit organization that provides curricular materials for educators teaching photography to young people. The organization is committed to art and cross-cultural exchange through community involvement.

Photovoice—www.photovoice.com

Photovoice enables people through photography to document their lives and communities, promote dialogue about personal and community issues, and reach policy makers.

YouthLearn—www.youthlearn.org

YouthLearn provides educators with resources and tools necessary to create technology-enhanced learning programs.

Notes

1. The curriculum used for the peace classes incorporated the Project YES curriculum, developed by Carole MacNeil and Beth Krensky, with courses created by the three Boys & Girls Club staff members facilitating the project.

2. The following is drawn from the YouthLearn curriculum and may be used in any community-art setting, with all ages, to teach photography. YouthLearn provides educators with the resources and tools necessary to create technology-enhanced learning programs. The web address for YouthLearn is www.youthlearn.org.

3. The following books provide excellent examples: Beth Krensky, with Neal Boyle, Roselyn Boyle, Patrick Gould, and Christen Rodriguez, *A Piece of Peace: Kids Share Their Lives through Poetry, Art & Photography* (Newton, Mass.: Font & Center Press, 1995) (available from www.project-yes.org); Wendy Ewald and Louise Neri, eds., *Towards a Promised Land* (London: Steidl Publishing, 2006); and Wendy Ewald, *Peace and Harmony: Carver Portraits* (New York: Distributed Art Publishers, 2006).

4. For detailed instructions on setting up a darkroom and the supplies needed, please see Wendy Ewald and Alexandra Lightfoot's *I Wanna Take Me a Picture: Teaching Photography and Writing to Children.*

5. Adobe's Photoshop and Photoshop Elements, Corel's Corel Photo-Paint, JASC Software's Paint Shop Pro, and Microsoft's PictureIt! are all commonly used photographic software packages.

6. Resin-coated and fiber-based papers are available in different grades—multigrade and fixed contrast—and different finishes—semi-gloss, matte, semi-matte, pearl, and others. Most educational darkrooms use resin-coated paper. If you plan to do your own processing and printing, refer to *I Wanna Take Me a Picture* for detailed information about the paper.

7. For more information about incorporating language with photographs, Ewald and Lightfoot's *I Wanna Take Me a Picture* is an excellent resource.

CHAPTER EIGHT

Graphics in Posters and Billboards, with Case Study by Juliet Biagi[1]

A Brief Art History of Posters and Billboards

Inscriptions and drawings on public walls date back to the beginning of recorded history and are considered "a universal part of human nature."[2] These public images and words form the foundation of graphic design. Because of their accessibility and potential for reproduction, the graphic arts, including posters and billboards, have the ability to reach a wide audience in community settings. Thus, graphic arts have been a core component to many social movements in the United States and throughout the world. The following case study illustrates a project in which youth were paired with a professional graphic designer to collaboratively create two large-scale bus posters. The chapter ends with a section on the essentials for effectively creating posters and billboards, followed by resources for the graphic-design process.

Project YES Case Study

About the Organization

Project YES, an acronym for Youth Envisioning Social change, creates leadership opportunities for youth through the arts and service learning. The organization supports diverse young people in using the arts as a tool for positive social change. (Chapter 6 provides additional information about Project YES.)

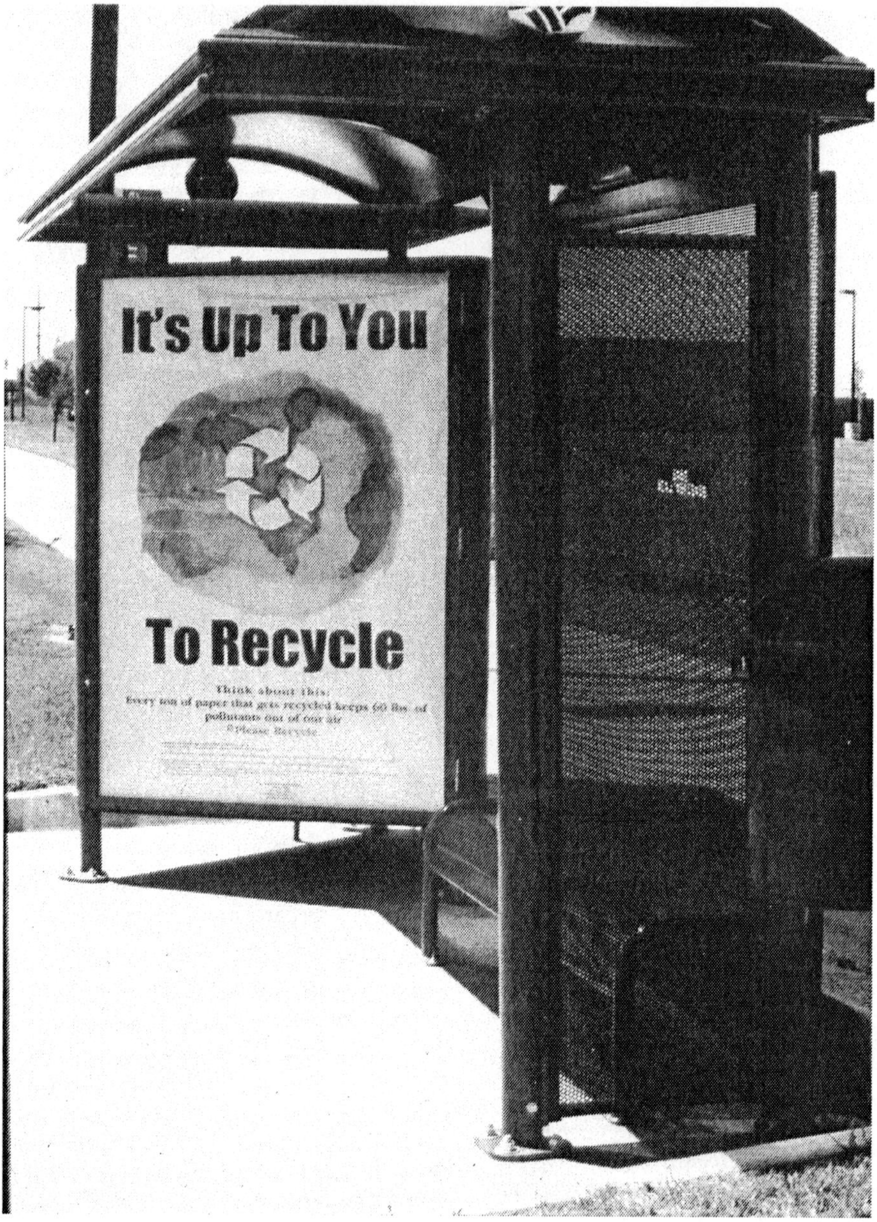

Figure 8.1. ***Recycling*** **poster displayed in bus shelter, 6' x 4', Project YES, Lafayette, Colorado, 1997.**

Photo credit: Carole MacNeil

A Community-Based Example: Bus Art Anti-Violence Posters

> "Our subject is very important because every two hours a child or teen will be killed by violence, and we want that to stop."
>
> —Comment from the Bus Art Workshop Youth Artist Statement

Shortly after the Columbine High School shootings in Littleton, Colorado, in 1999, Project YES held a workshop with middle-school-age youth in Lafayette, Colorado, to create a piece of public art about a critical community issue. A group of eight diverse middle-school-age young people used graphic arts to create two large posters addressing handgun violence and youth that were displayed on the sides of four public buses for six weeks.[3]

Workshop Process

Introductions and community building: The workshop began with a group discussion about community and common expectations. The co-leaders asked the youth, "What do we need to become and stay a community?" and "What do we do when we don't agree?" The youth determined ground rules for their workshop and engaged in community-building games and activities that helped them to learn about themselves and others. Each workshop day concluded with an affirmation session "to reaffirm to the kids that they are important and they are making a difference in the community."

Issue exploration and selection: The group then discussed what social issues were and brainstormed a list of possible social issues that were relevant to them for the art project, including violence, guns, drugs, and pollution. After conducting interviews in the community asking "How does each issue impact our community?" the youth agreed that handgun violence was the most urgent issue. After further discussion to narrow the topic, the group decided to focus on handgun violence against youth. The youth stated, "We came up with the subject because that has been a problem. We want to show that we care about all the kids that have been killed from violence."

Poster design: Such mini-art projects as collages about social issues provided opportunities for youth to experience the artistic brainstorming process and to look at how images are effective in conveying different messages. David Underwood, a professional graphic designer from the University of Colorado, Boulder, was invited to work as a collaborating artist on the project and worked with the group on two occasions. David talked about what graphic designers do, where design can be seen (products, signs, advertising), how designers work (concept, design, production), and the elements of good design. The youth discussed the intended audience and message for the posters before starting individual sketches, and they were encouraged to experiment with combining words and images in their designs. The youth then critiqued one another's sketches.

Poster creation: The group selected two youths' sketches to build on as a group. Together, they determined that one poster would include photographs of each youth in the workshop with the written words "Stop the violence, let's be friends" and the statistic "every two hours a child or teen is killed by gunfire." The second poster would include words and graphics only, reading "Stop the violence, PEACE is possible" and the statistic just noted. Sarah Petty, a graphic designer and one of the two workshop co-leaders, put the group's designs into digital format. The posters were then printed by a digital printing company through a Denver transit advertising business, developing enough copies for display and one for each youth to keep.

Unveiling/celebration: Following one of the most tragic events in Colorado's history, the community-art workshop provided an opportunity for young people to address the issue of gun violence and youth in their own community in a constructive manner. The youth unveiled their posters to the community at an event held at the Lafayette Public Library. They invited a local city council member to speak with them on the importance of the project and their message. The youth discussed their group process, the creation of their art, and what they gained from the workshop. The local press attended the event and published a story in the *Lafayette News* titled "No to violence, YES to peace." The two posters were then displayed on four local buses, at the Lafayette Public Library, at the Project YES Youth Center, and on a Peace Bus that traveled around the island of Hawaii.

Collaboration

Lafayette Public Library provided space for the workshops as well as resources for the youth to research their topic. As noted earlier, David Underwood offered an overview of effective design principles and Sarah Petty provided critical technical assistance. David helped the students understand the relationship between concept and design, put more "punch" into their work, and acted as the bridge between the students' creative processes and the technical demands of taking the projects to press. David felt that he helped to challenge and focus the students and offered the technical guidance needed for those unfamiliar with graphic arts. The Regional Transportation District (RTD) provided advertising space on its buses at a discounted rate, allowing the youth's art to be widely viewed in the community. RTD representatives were so excited about the project and the quality of the posters that they extended the display time on the buses at no additional charge.

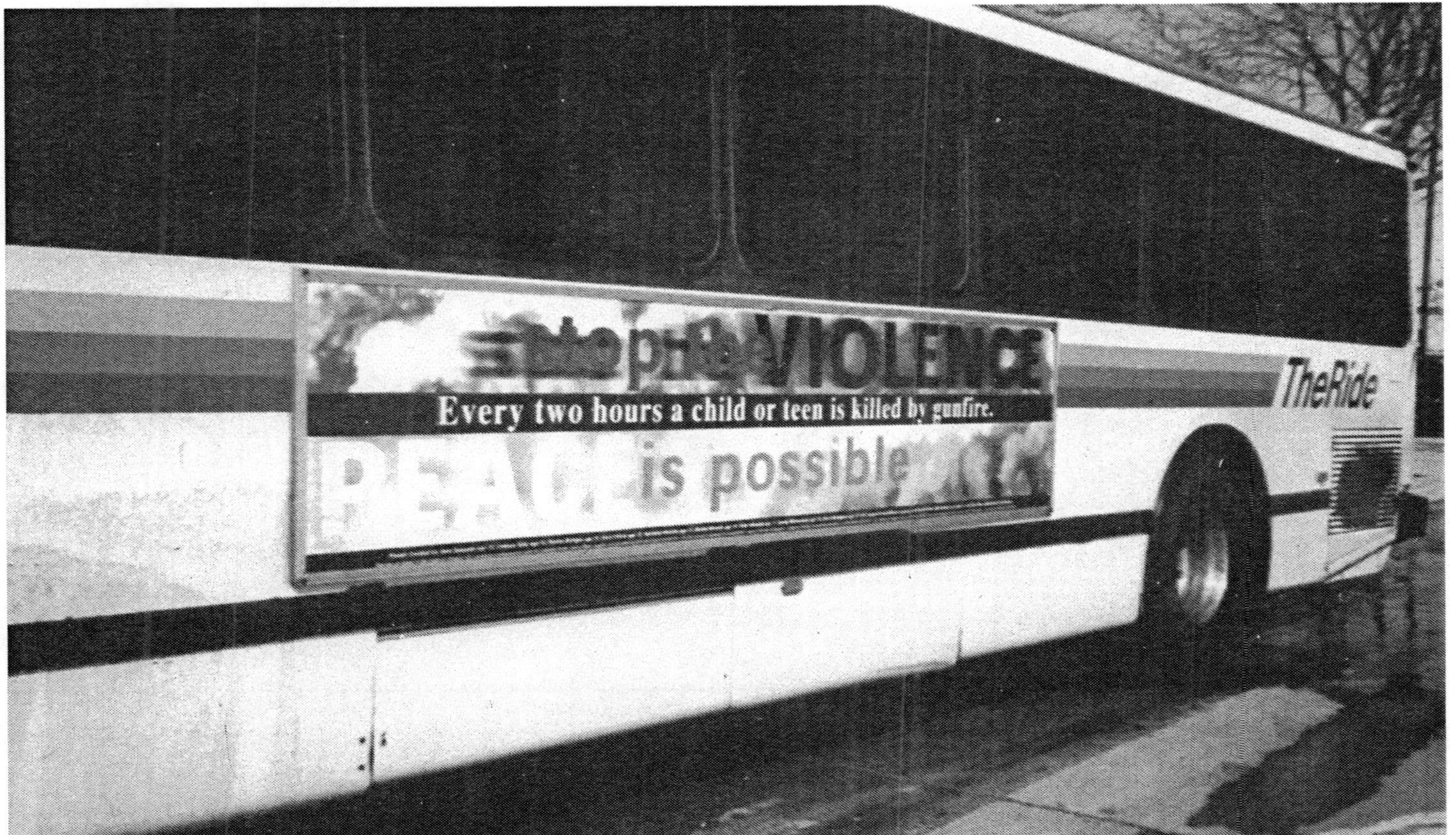

Figure 8.2. ***Bus Art Anti-Violence*** **poster, 12' x 3', Project YES, Lafayette, Colorado, 1999.**
Photo credit: Carole MacNeil

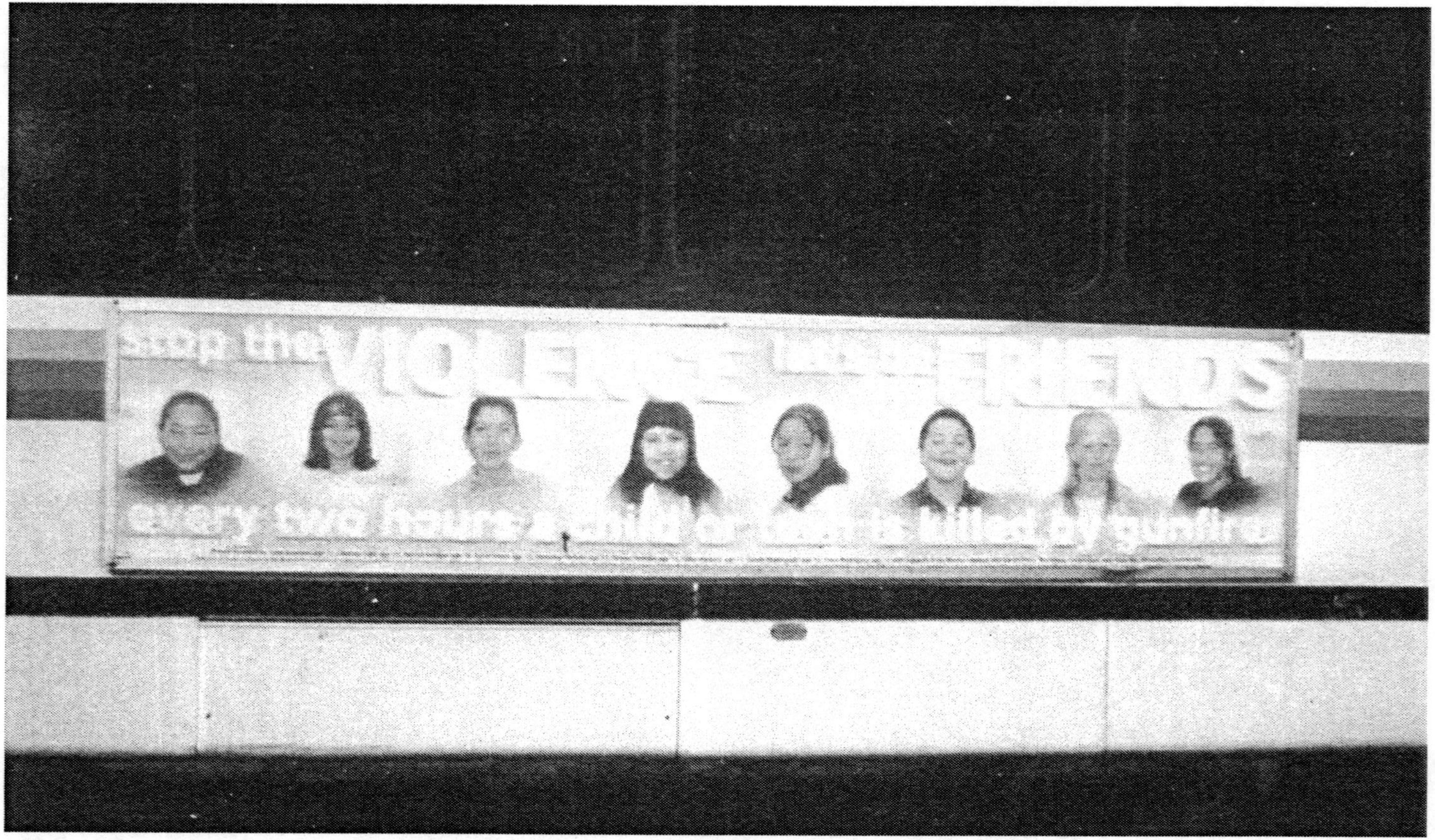

Figure 8.3. ***Bus Art Anti-Violence*** **poster, 12' x 3', Project YES, Lafayette, Colorado, 1999.**
Photo credit: Carole MacNeil

Three Essential Elements of This Project

1. Having a graphic designer as the co-leader allowed artistic concepts and guidance to be present throughout the entire workshop and provided for the transfer of the youth's designs to a graphic format.
2. Showing the youth examples of other youth-created posters inspired them to think about their own project's possibilities.
3. The use of the graphic arts medium and the display of the art on public buses were extremely powerful for the youth. They were thrilled to see buses passing by with their picture and message. As the art travelled between towns on the buses, the youth's art gained excellent exposure.

Important Things to Remember

While it was necessary in this case for the co-leader to create the graphic designs for the posters using the youth's images, the youth would ideally have access to the needed technology so they might personally engage in the digital-art process as much as possible. In addition, with community-art projects like this one, a need exists to look beyond students' lack of visual fluency to the core of their ideas and help them make those ideas sing. Lastly, adults should sublimate their own natural tendencies to take over.

Essentials for Creating Posters and Billboards

Please refer to chapter 2 for an overview of the community-art process that we suggest as a framework. If you are planning a community-based poster or billboard, we strongly recommend collaborating with a professional graphic designer and using the recommended resources to gain an in-depth understanding of the graphic design process. Below are the essential components we suggest for creating a poster or billboard.[4]

Designing a Poster

- Understand the intent. Posters are used to announce an event; promote a person, place, or thing; sell an item; or develop or change an attitude or characteristic.[5] Successful posters convey "simple ideas which communicate instantly, yet somehow stay in the mind."[6] They are not intended to be simplistic but, rather, send a message that engages and involves the viewer and starts a dialogue.
- Teach basic design theory so the participants can make informed decisions about the creation and critique of their work. As foundational skills for graphic design work, Shin and Proctor suggest teaching the three areas of *visual hierarchy*, *design principles*, and *typography*.[7]

- *Visual hierarchy* relates to the hierarchy of the information, typically images and text, found in the piece.[8] Designers use color, value, position, shape, and size to establish a visual hierarchy. Participants should consider the visual flow when designing the piece. The arrangement of the visual elements and type helps facilitate this flow. Additionally, once the participants decide which information is the most important to convey, they should use the criteria of color, value, position, shape, and size to influence where on the poster a viewer will look first, second, third, and so on.
- Understanding *design principles* is necessary to create successful posters.[9] Given that graphic design "is a direct and clear communication of a message using visuals and words,"[10] graphic designer Robin Williams[11] suggests that *proximity*, *repetition*, *contrast*, and *alignment* are critical principles to apply.
    - *Proximity* means grouping related items near each other so they can be seen as one visual unit rather than numerous separate units. This will help to reduce visual clutter.
    - *Repetition* may be used to repeat elements of design. Line, shape, color, texture, size, direction, and value may be repeated throughout the piece.
    - *Contrast* is used to enhance and highlight difference.
    - *Alignment* makes a piece more cohesive. Placement of all visual elements should be purposeful, not arbitrary; each item should be visually connected to something else on the page.
- *Typography* concerns the effective use of type—fonts and type sizes. Typography choices are not arbitrary but, rather, informed by considering the size, weight, structure, form, and color of the font. The type of font and its placement impact the piece significantly: "Good design cannot be made by randomly placing words composed of any fonts anywhere on a design project."[12] Contrast may be created by combining significantly different sizes and weights of typeface. Participants also should become familiar with the different categories of type, such as old style, modern, slab serif, sans serif, script, and decorative. An introductory book on design can provide a good overview, with examples of these different categories.

- Understand *color theory*. According to Bernstein,[13] it also is important to choose colors with high contrast, consider the meanings with which colors are imbued, and choose colors for their receding or advancing qualities. Placing complementary colors adjacent to each other creates high contrast, as does combining yellow and black. It is important to consider the figure–ground relationship, that is, the relationship of the subject or figure to the ground or surrounding field. Black text on a white ground, or vice versa, creates the contrast needed for a viewer to read it clearly. Participants can explore the different results that occur when placing colors with different hues, values, and intensities next to each other to determine successful contrast levels.

Designing a Billboard

- Although billboard design should adhere to the aforementioned principles, billboards differ from posters in terms of scale, proximity, and viewing time. While viewers can spend more time examining posters, a billboard is viewed for no longer than an average of thirty to forty-five seconds.[14] The image and message should be clear and simple, allowing a viewer to "get it" quickly. Colors should have more contrast than posters in order to add to the simplicity. In *Advertising Outdoors: Watch This Space!*,[15] David Bernstein outlines rules, displayed in Table 8.1, to be used for designing billboards[16]:

Table 8.1. Rules for Designing Billboards

Simplicity	Allow nothing elaborate, ornate, or complicated in the design or verbal message
One dominant image	This can be a collision or fusion of two images. Indeed, many famous posters communicate two thoughts by means of a visual or verbal pun.
Boldness	Make the image and message stand out. Do not be subtle.
Clean, legible type	Light or delicate lettering, closely spaced type, or type superimposed upon a complicated background does not work at great heights.
Few words	Use no more than six or seven words—for immediate impact. If there are more, the sentences should be short.
Large-enough type	Type should be large enough to read from the specific distance for the particular site. Billboard companies recommend that letters be a minimum of one foot tall—and a minimum of two feet tall for an audience more than sixty-five years old.
Contrasting colors	Preferably, primary colors should be used. Again, this is not the place for subtle nuances.
Brand	Ensure not simply that the logo is large enough but also that the entire design belongs to the brand. Keep in mind that this rule is particular to a product or organization that has a logo. Disregard this rule if it does not apply to your project. The logo of the product or agency should be visibly linked to the ad, or it will simply be overlooked.

Printing Posters or Billboards

As mentioned earlier, posters and billboards can be created by designing them on paper and scanning the completed image or by digitally creating the design and layout.[17] There are some commonly used graphic design and layout programs that can assist with digitally creating the design.[18] Work may be printed on paper or other materials, such as silk or vinyl. When outsourcing the printing, one should first contact the printer, billboard company, or transit authority to comply with any specifications for preparing a digital file.

Avoiding Risks

- Design a poster or billboard for the intended audience. Remember that the piece does not need to appeal to everyone.
- Keep the design simple. Often, collaborative projects include multiple designs in one composition. This is difficult for viewers to decipher quickly and can result in the poster or billboard being ignored.
- Remember that "less is more." Keep fonts and colors simple so that the poster or billboard is legible.

Please refer to the following print and web-based resources for more information about the history and process of graphic design.

Graphic Design Resources

Case Study Contact Information

Project YES
200 E. South Boulder Rd. Ste C2, Lafayette, CO 80026
(303) 926-0306
www.project-yes.org

Print Resources

Bernstein, David. *Advertising Outdoors: Watch This Space!* New York: Phaidon, 1997.

Landa, Robin. *Graphic Design Solutions.* Albany, N.Y.: On Word Press, 2001.

Lewandowsky, Pina, and Francis Zeischegg. *A Practical Guide to Digital Design: Designing With Your Computer Made Easy!* Lausanne, Switzerland: AVA Publishing SA, 2003.

Shin, Seung-Ruyl, and Marilyn Proctor. "Teaching Computer Graphic Design." *National Art Education Association Advisory* (Summer 2005): 1.

Steward Heon, Laura, Peggy Diggs, and Lisa Dorin. *Billboard Art on the Road.* North Adams, Mass.: MASS MoCA Publications, 1999.

Sullivan, Luke. *Hey Whipple Squeeze This: A Guide to Creating Great Ads*. Somerset, N.J.: John Wiley & Sons, Inc., 2003.

Williams, Robin. *The Non-Designer's Design Book*. Berkeley, Calif.: Peachpit Press, 1994.

Web Resources

The Kennedy Center ArtsEdge—artsedge.kennedy-center.org

This site includes numerous lesson plans on graphic design and poster creation. The "Olympic Posters" lesson plan offers a handout on "Characteristics and Concepts for Posters." The "Poster and Press" lesson plan outlines a process for helping students design a poster.

Cooper-Hewitt National Design Museum Educator Resource Center—www.educatorresourcecenter.org

This site includes numerous interdisciplinary graphic design lesson plans for all ages. The site also lists multiple web resources.

Notes

1. Information in this case study includes contributions from Carole MacNeil, Sara Nix, and David Underwood.

2. Kurt Varnedoe and Blake Gopnick, *Modern Art and Popular Culture: Readings in High and Low* (New York: Harry N. Abrams, 1990), 69.

3. The Project YES curriculum used for the Bus Art project was developed by Carole MacNeil and Beth Krensky between 1990 and 2000.

4. Irina Zadov, an artist and community art educator based in Chicago, provided initial information about the essentials for creating posters and billboards.

5. This information comes from "Characteristics and Concepts for Posters," an online handout for students developed by ArtsEdge.net (please see Graphic Design Resources above).

6. Bernstein, David, *Advertising Outdoors: Watch This Space!* (New York: Phaidon, 1997), 72.

7. The following information on visual hierarchy, design principles, and typography are from Seung-Ruyl Shin and Marilyn Proctor, "Teaching Computer Graphic Design," *National Art Education Association Advisory* (Summer 2005): 1.

8. This information is found in Robin Landa's *Graphic Design Solutions* (see Graphic Design Resources above). Please see this work for further information and ideas about visual hierarchy.

9. David Bernstein provides a strong overview of the history, rules, and creation of billboards in *Advertising Outdoors: Watch This Space!*

10. Shin and Proctor, "Teaching Computer Graphic Design," 1.

11. Robin Williams, *The Non-Designer's Design Book, Third Edition* (Berkeley: Peachpit Press, 2005), 14.

12. Shin and Proctor, "Teaching Computer Graphic Design," 2.

13. Bernstein, *Advertising Outdoors: Watch This Space!*, 74.

14. Bernstein, *Advertising Outdoors: Watch This Space!*, 79.

15. We strongly recommend David Bernstein's *Advertising Outdoors: Watch This Space!* for an overview of the history and production of billboards as well as numerous examples of successful posters and billboards. A good resource for creating posters and billboards digitally is *A Practical Guide to Digital Design: Designing With Your Computer Made Easy!* by Lewandowsky and Zeischegg (please see Graphic Design Resources above).

16. Bernstein, *Advertising Outdoors: Watch This Space!*, 73.

17. A good resource for creating posters and billboards digitally is *A Practical Guide to Digital Design: Designing With Your Computer Made Easy!* by Lewandowsky and Zeischegg (please see Graphic Design Resources above).

18. The following graphic design and layout programs are recommended by Shin and Proctor in "Teaching Computer Graphic Design": Photoshop, Illustrator, and Freehand (graphic design); InDesign, Quark Express, and PageMaker (layout).

CHAPTER NINE

Video by Irina Zadov, with Case Study by Matt Bradley

A Brief Art History of Video

Like film, video records live action by capturing motion and sound digitally or analogically. Video allows participants to create films, document personal events, and share their thoughts and ideas with a wider audience. Video cameras can capture footage that few people have access to and broadcast the footage to many. The medium also allows numerous participants to work collaboratively to plan, shoot, and edit a piece, making it well suited to community-based art projects. The following case study illustrates how a youth media center facilitated a community-based video documentary project with area youth. Following the case study, the essentials for planning and creating a video, and resources for video production, are discussed.

Spy Hop Productions Video Documentary Case Study

About the Organization

Spy Hop Productions, a not-for-profit youth media center based in Salt Lake City, Utah, is committed to cultivating the visions and voices of an emerging generation via the big screen, the airwaves, and the World Wide Web.

Spy Hop Productions offers after-school and summer programming for K–12 participants in video production (documentary and narrative), animation (3D, clay, and Flash), sound engineering, and web design. After-school and summer film projects, from intensive week-long programs to year-long commitments, have ranged from documentaries capturing the 2002 Winter Olympics through teenage eyes, to subtitled farces profiling distressed Frenchmen, to Claymation shorts capturing the anguish of a shepherd at shearing time. Also produced in the Spy Hop sound room are original movie scores, solo and band recordings, and radio documentaries.

Spy Hop Productions' unique programming specializes in educational solutions through the multimedia arts. Dedicated to providing hands-on experiences, the organization offers training in the technical and creative aspects of multimedia production. Spy Hop Productions' unique Youth Documentary Arts Program (YDAP) enables youth to explore pertinent stories and issues while developing a variety of skills and abilities. Documentary work is a creative medium that allows youth to become civically and critically involved while expressing their views and sharing their stories and those of others. YDAP provides youth with the opportunity to work with experienced mentors and documentarians to create their own video and audio documentaries. Participants are immersed in the practical and theoretical aspects of documentary work. The program enables participants to develop and hone innovative processes and technical skills in a number of areas, including story development, the creative process, nonfiction filmmaking styles, camera operation, cinematography, and editing. In addition, participants develop such ethnographic skills as interviewing and participant observation while addressing an array of ethical questions and issues.

A Community-Based Example: "Kainga Malosi: *'Auhia Kae Kisu Atu Pe: a journey against the tides*"

In 2004 a group of Pacific Islander youth, participating in the Spy Hop Productions Youth Documentary Arts Program, produced a thirty-minute video documentary that explored the educational experiences of Pacific Islanders living along the Wasatch Front in Utah. The youth worked with filmmakers and media educators 'Amelia Niumeitolu and Matt Bradley to identify education as the issue they chose to address; conduct research; and then plan, produce, and distribute their film. The film premiered at Salt Lake City Public Library and has since been used in classrooms, screened at educational conferences, and shown to the Utah State Board of Education.

The young filmmakers describe who they are and the nature of their project in these words:

> We are all Pacific Islanders who came from different places and are involved with the Youth Documentary Arts Program at Spy Hop Productions. We chose to call ourselves Kainga Malosi to reflect our culture and our goals. The word

Kainga originates from the Tongan word meaning extended family and community. The word *Malosi* hails from Samoa and is defined as strength, energy, and power because we are finding ways to make our communities stronger. We have been doing research and interviews to find some of the strengths of our Pacific Islander community, as well as some of the weaknesses. We are looking for ways to use our strengths to address our weaknesses.

Through our interviews and research we decided to focus on education as our main topic, specifically drop-out rates, test scores, and further education among Pacific Islanders. We want to find out why many Pacific Islanders are dropping out of high school and have low test scores.

We hope that we can change the lives of our generation and the generations to come in the future. We are doing this to help our community come together, raise our expectations about our education, and ensure that Pacific Islander youth take education seriously. We want to let the world know that we have a voice.

Pre-Workshop Process

Spy Hop Productions worked with the Salt Lake Community Action Program and Horizonte Instruction and Training Center to recruit youth from a Pacific Islander club at Horizonte. The majority of the youth involved came from this group, but Spy Hop also attracted some youth from local high schools by meeting with their Pacific Islander clubs. Spy Hop staff members created fliers to distribute at the meetings and also took pizza and a sign-up sheet when they met with the student clubs at the schools.

Workshop Process

Pre-production: One of Spy Hop's first actions was to show some previously youth-produced documentaries to motivate the young people. Spy Hop then began identifying with the youth both strengths and weaknesses in their community so that it could then determine how the community's strengths could be applied to address the problems. Spy Hop used various brainstorming, mapping, and video interviewing exercises in thinking about these topics. As Spy Hop worked toward narrowing the many subject areas to one topic that would become the focus of the documentary, it also did "street surveys" at various sites in the community. After approximately forty street surveys, Spy Hop staff members reviewed the results and identified the community members' major concerns. Education, which the youth had also identified as a concern in initial conversations, topped the list. Specifically, the youth were concerned about the greater-than-average high school drop-out rates and low standardized test scores in the Pacific Islander community. With education as the topic of focus, the youth then began the process of setting up longer, more detailed

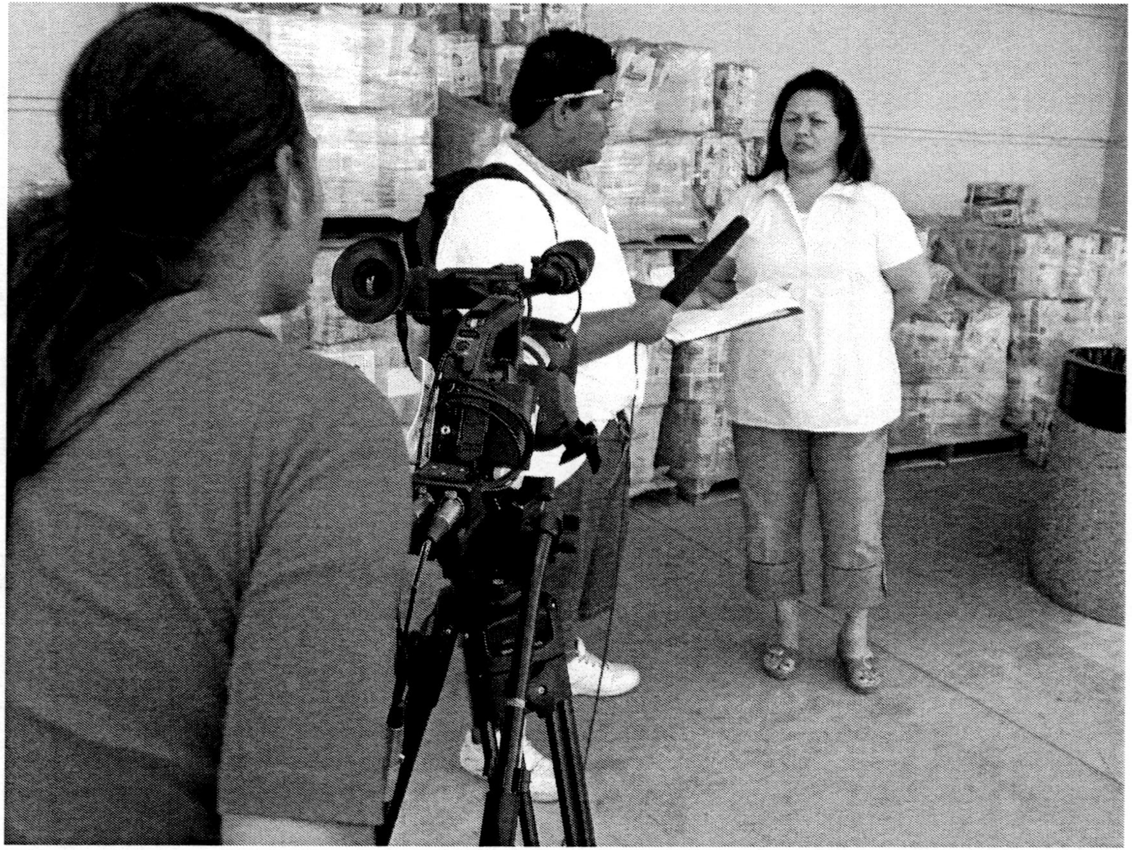

Figure 9.1. "Kainga Malosi: *'Auhia Kae Kisu Atu Pe: a journey against the tides'*" video, Spy Hop Productions, Salt Lake City, Utah, 2004.

interviews with community members that would focus more on the educational experiences of Pacific Islanders in Utah.

Production: The group spent significant time writing interview questions, practicing interview techniques, using the camera equipment, and filming community events to get B-roll (which adds contextually relevant video to illustrate the story). The youth sought to interview community members from the many different islands (Maori, Samoan, Tongan, Hawaiian, Fijian, etc.) and also to interview people who were doing well in school as well as those who had dropped out. To put the experiences of participants, parents, and others interviewed into perspective, they also interviewed Pacific Islanders who were actively involved in the public school system as teachers, counselors, or administrators as well as some doctoral participants who were conducting research about Pacific Islander educational experiences and epistemologies. One of the youth's early decisions was to let Pacific Islanders tell their story, and as a result they focused specifically on interviewing Pacific Islanders. They also wanted to focus on youth, but finding youth who had dropped out of high school and were willing to be videotaped about their experiences proved to be quite challenging. The youth conducted approximately twenty-five to thirty interviews and filmed a variety of other community events.

In addition to conducting interviews, the youth began to think about how to best "tell their story." Project mentor 'Amelia Niumeitolu worked closely with the youth to identify culturally specific ways they could communicate some of the important concepts of their documentary. 'Amelia and the youth determined that they wanted to use island proverbs to frame different parts of the documentary and then spoke at length with elders, family members, and others to hear the proverbs and their meanings. The title of the film itself was derived from one such proverb. The group also discussed how to provide the background for the story and set the stage. They decided to create a story about a young woman who could represent many of their stories and wrote narration about this young woman. The participants discussed who would play the role and then developed shot lists that could accompany the narration. The "composite story" that emerged served as an introduction and conclusion to the many interviews included in the final video piece.

Post-production: Editing proved to be one of the project's most challenging aspects. The youth had developed great camera, cinematography, and interview skills, but because of time restraints and the approaching deadline for the screening, not all of the youth had time to learn all of the editing skills needed to work on the final piece. As a result, project mentor Matt Bradley did most of the actual editing, based on what the youth determined should be included

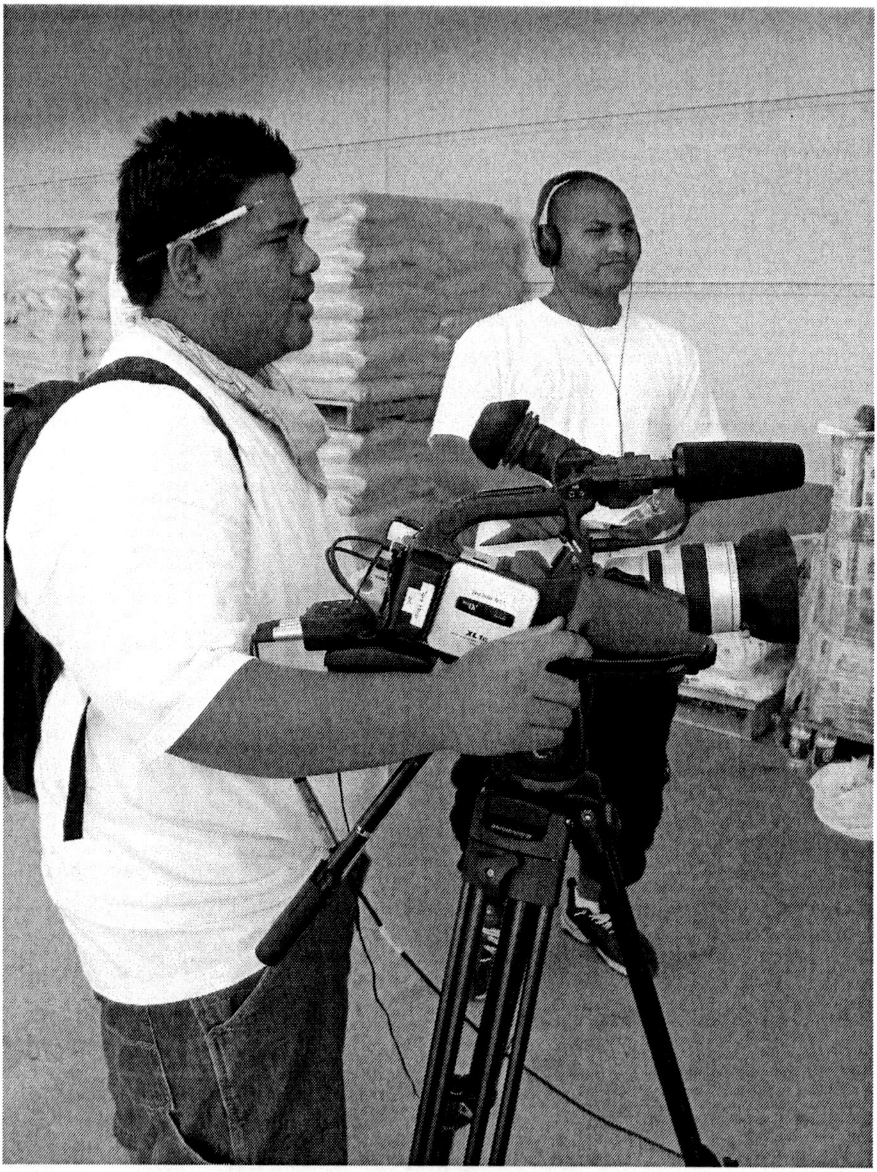

Figure 9.2. "Kainga Malosi: *'Auhia Kae Kisu Atu Pe: a journey against the tides'*" filmmakers, Spy Hop Productions, Salt Lake City, Utah, 2004.

in the final video. The youth spent hours logging all of the tapes they had shot and identifying the important, consistent themes they thought were important to address. They decided to present an alternative to the often-used portrayal of Pacific Islanders as not interested in education or not motivated. As a result, they found many stories of Pacific Islander youth talking about their educational successes and their parents' involvement in their education. The youth decided to also include sections addressing the discrimination many of them experienced and the notion of *fie palangi* (to "act white," or be "whitewashed") and how both of those topics related to their educational experiences.

As the youth determined the themes to address and the specific clips and interviews to use, Matt assembled them in the editing timeline. The youth watched the rough video in different formats and provided critiques about what they liked and did not like. As Matt worked on the editing, 'Amelia helped the youth write and record final narration to be added as "voice-over" to different sections of the video.

Throughout the various stages of the process, project mentors 'Amelia and Matt provided instruction and training in video production skills, educational theories, media literacy and criticism, and culturally specific materials. 'Amelia arranged for many guest speakers to talk about the history and culture of the Pacific Islands, and the participants read and discussed Pacific Islander poets and writers as well as short articles and commentary on education. They learned how to research statistics and data about education, test scores, and related information that comes to bear on educational achievement.

Screening and Outreach

The youth planned and hosted a final screening of their video documentary at Salt Lake City Public Library. They created fliers that were posted around town at food markets, libraries, and schools, and they wrote and e-mailed invitations to school district superintendents, principals, and other state and district school administrators. Each of the youth hand-delivered invitations to their own teachers, principals, community leaders, and parents, and they promoted the screening during a local, live Pacific Islanders public affairs radio program.

For the world premiere screening, many of the youth prepared talks that dealt with education and were based on some of the proverbs they had collected. The youth discussed the process of creating the film and then presented gifts to their parents and other community members who helped support the project. After showing the film, they held a question-and-answer session to discuss the issues raised in the film or the production of the film.

As a result of the screening, the youth received numerous invitations to show the film in a variety of contexts, including the Utah Council on Conflict Resolution, a Pacific Islander–American Experience course taught at the University of Utah, Pacific Islander Awareness Week at Salt Lake Community College, a Pacific Islander Education Conference at Brigham Young University, the Utah Board of Education, and the Salt Lake City School District Superintendent.

Reflection

In the crunch of completing the film, Spy Hop did not prepare the participants sufficiently for the question-and-answer session; while they did their best, many of them felt very uncomfortable. The participants had been researching and documenting issues relevant to Pacific Islanders and education for approximately one year. The youth involved developed more than six months of experience with different aspects of documentary film production, including interviewing, cinematography, researching, and editing. Through their training at Spy Hop Productions, they gained the skills to film in a variety of environments, from interview settings to community events.

Kainga Malosi youth will create a second documentary video through their involvement with the Youth Documentary Arts Program (YDAP) at Spy Hop Productions. To date, they have conducted more than twenty interviews and filmed a variety of events, including public meetings, the king of Tonga's visit to Utah, and the Samoan Flag Day Festival. The youth will shoot reflective video journals, interviews, screenings, and discussions as well as footage of their daily activities as they attempt to organize and complete projects regarding their education. This footage will be edited to create a second video to complement their first piece.

The following section provides a brief overview of the essential components for producing a video.

Essentials for the Video Production Process

Please refer to chapter 2 for an overview of the community-art process that we suggest as a framework. If you are planning a community-based video production, we strongly recommend collaborating with a professional videographer and using the recommended resources to gain an in-depth understanding of the video production process. Below are the essential components for creating a video using the context of documentary production as a guide.

The following overview uses the documentary genre to outline the process for planning and creating a video.[1]

Pre-Production

Once a topic has been chosen and the appropriate research has been conducted, the group should agree upon the type of video to create. The group should create a storyboard with the following essential components: the action of the characters in a scene; the placement of the camera and lights; information about transitions, special effects, dialogue, narration, and sound track; content; placement, font, and size of text; graphics; and background color.

Production

While pre-production is the preparatory stage of video, production is the actual shooting of the tape. This process can take place either in a studio or on location. Production recommendations are as follow:

- Make sure all necessary equipment is available and tested. A checklist of equipment might include:
    - Camera with extra tapes and batteries
    - Light meter/grey card
    - Tripod/dolly/crane
    - Lights, gels, reflectors, extra bulbs
    - Microphones (specific ones for the set and backups)
    - Headphones
    - Extension cords (Stingers)
    - Clothespins (C-42s)
- Plan what kind of footage is necessary for the specific locations. If shot on location, lighting is very important because natural light changes and shots taken at different times may not match up in color. Natural or daytime lighting works best for camcorders. When digital cameras are set on automatic, they will adjust to the lightest part of the room.
- Create a shooting schedule. This involves scheduling dates and times for the shoot, including interviews. All schedule information should be logged along with the type of equipment and crew, and the location, needed for that day. On a day before the shoot occurs, check the set location at the scheduled time of day to make sure the lighting and sound will be appropriate.
- Choose the appropriate shot for the needed footage. Table 9.1 lists some different types of shots.
- Select an appropriate microphone for the highest quality sound. While many producers focus on image quality, sound is just as important to the

Table 9.1. Types of Shots

Zoom	One of the most basic and easiest-to-understand features of a camcorder is the zoom-in button. While this tool can be useful, it should be used sparingly, as too much zooming will distract from a shot. The effect of zoom flattens the space, whereas physically bringing the camera closer keeps the proper perspective.
Close up	The close up (CU) shows something in detail. When referring to a person, the close up shot captures the head and shoulders.
Extreme close up	The extreme close up, on the other hand, is significantly closer, like a shot of a person's eye or mouth. When using this feature, remember that even the slightest movement will shake the camera. Use a tripod for these shots.
Medium shot	The medium shot (MS) is useful for an interview situation because it shows the upper torso of the interviewee as well as his or her surroundings. This shot is also helpful because it is easier to follow the subject.
Long shot	The long shot (LS) is taken from a distance and shows a broad view of a scene rather than detail. This shot is good for setting a scene or for showing a large group of people. The distance on this shot will create more focus and camera movements will not be as obvious.
Establishing shot	The establishing shot, which is usually a long shot, is used to inform the viewer about the contents of the next scene. For instance, if the outside of a restaurant is shown, the viewer will understand why the people in the next shot are eating.
Cutaway, or cover shot	The cutaway, or cover shot, is used to cover a jump cut edit. This shot will be a short clip related to the words being spoken and is intended to hide the change of the face when a certain part of the interview is cut out.
Panoramic shot	The panoramic (pan) shot scans the area to show a broader view of the scene. This shot is created when the camera is moved from one side to the other. This effect works best when the camera remains focused on one object, slowly moves to the other side, and then holds still on another object.
Tilt shot	The tilt shot occurs when the camera is moved from top to bottom or bottom to top. This method is useful for capturing tall objects or lengthy distances. This shot should be done slowly so all of the details are captured with the camera movements.

finished product. Use headphones to monitor the sound being recorded. Table 9.2 outlines types of microphones.

Post-Production

Post-production refers to everything that is done to the video after it has been shot. The major portion of this work is editing. Editing recommendations are as follow:

Table 9.2. Types of Microphones

Shotgun	The best microphones for interviews are unidirectional or shotgun microphones, which pick up sound only from the top, keeping the outside noise from interfering with the speaker's clarity. However, it is important to keep the microphone pointed in the speaker's direction so it does not pick up any additional sound.
Cardioid	The cardioid microphone picks up sound from the top and from the sides. It works best in an interior setting with little background noise and near the mouth of the speaker.
Omnidirectional	The omnidirectional microphone is best for picking up environmental sound. It records sound from all directions and works great for B-roll footage and establishing shots. One thing to remember about these microphones is to keep them away from the camera and crew so that their sounds are not recorded. In addition, when shooting outside, remember to bring a wind screen that can be placed over the microphone to muffle the sound of the wind. Camcorder microphones are usually omnidirectional.

- Editing determines what the final product will look like. When editing, keep in mind the goals and main ideas of the video. What should be done to ensure that the intended message is the received message? In what order should the information be presented to have the greatest impact? How should the audience feel after watching the film? The main components of editing include:
  - Rearranging the sequence of events
  - Adding titles, credits, narration, and music

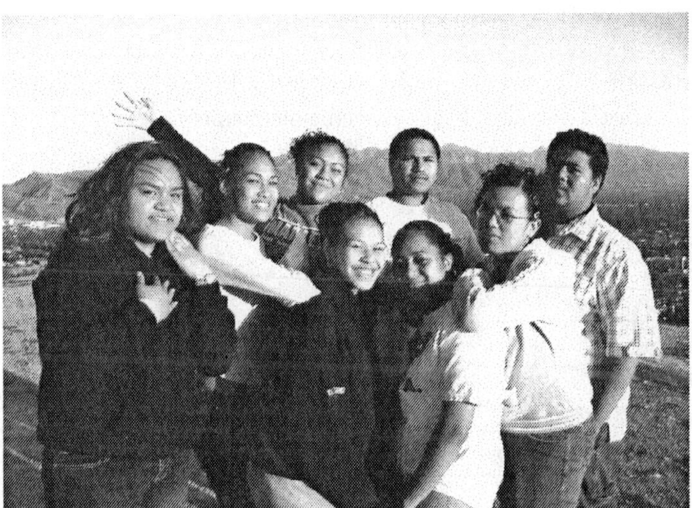

Figure 9.3. "Kainga Malosi: '*Auhia Kae Kisu Atu Pe: a journey against the tides*'" filmmakers, Spy Hop Productions, Salt Lake City, Utah, 2004.

  - Using the best shots or sequences
  - Making some parts longer or shorter
  - Correcting bad sound or audio
  - Combining audio and video
  - Stating and reinforcing ideas
  - Creating a mood or moods
  - Comparing different points of views through juxtaposition
- The technical component of editing can be done in several different ways.[2] The most common editing method used by professionals is through digital film editing software. If such applications are not available, VHS tapes may be merged to make one final product.
- Logging the footage is the first step of editing. The main information that should be logged is the video's quality and content, the audio's quality and content, which shots need to be retaken, and which shots may be cut. Table 9.3 illustrates a typical log sheet.
- A final edit may be created after a paper edit is completed. This involves writing the sequence of shots as the group wants them to appear in the finished video.

Avoiding Risks

- Ensure that each person recorded in the video signs a consent form that legally allows his or her footage to be used; otherwise, completion and screening of the video may be delayed, sometimes indefinitely. In addition, providing everyone included in the video with an information sheet containing the video's purpose and the production group's contact information, may be helpful.
- Lighting is an important aspect of a successful video. Digital film, in particular, is sensitive to light and cannot handle extreme changes. For this reason, one should pay careful attention to the lighting. Footage

Table 9.3. Log Sheet

Title: Neighborhood Clean-Up
Location: Park

Time	*Video Description*	*Audio Description*	*Comments*
0:00–0:30	Color bars	None	None
0:30–1:30	Wide shot of boy picking up trash	None	Shot looks good, can be used
1:30–2:0	Head and shoulder shot of boy	Sounds of birds singing	Shaky camera, cannot be used

taken outdoors in the same location should be shot at the same time of day to allow for continuity when combining shots.

- Check all equipment before a shoot, and monitor audio and video during a shoot. Most videographers have had the experience of not capturing an important shot because of technical difficulties. Often, these difficulties can be prevented with simple precautions.

Please refer to the following print and web-based resources for more information about the history and process of producing videos.

Video Resources

Case Study Contact Information

Spy Hop Productions
511 West 200 South, Suite 100
Salt Lake City, UT 84101
(801) 532-7500
www.spyhop.org

Print Resources

Avid Technologies. *Editing with Avid Xpress Pro*. New York: Peachpit Press, 2003.

Carlson, Jeff. *Making a Movie in iMovie HD and iDVD 5: Visual QuickProject Guide (Visual QuickProject Series)*. New York: Peachpit Press, 2005.

Flynn, Deras. *Guide to Creating Digital Video Like a Pro*. Indianapolis: Que. Series TechTV, 2002.

Geduld, Marcus. *Premiere Pro Editing Workshop*. New York: CMP Books, 2004.

Goodman, Steven. *Teaching Youth Media. A Critical Guide to Literacy, Video Production, and Social Change*. New York: Teacher's College Press, 2003.

Greenwood, Daniel. *Action! In the Classroom. A Guide to Student Produced Video in K–12 Education*. Oxford, U.K.: The Scarecrow Press, Inc., 2003.

Kawin, Bruce, and Gerald Mast. *A Short History of the Movies. Eighth Edition*. Upper Saddle River, N.J.: Pearson Education Inc., 2003.

Kobler, Helmut. *Final Cut Pro HD for Dummies*. New York: For Dummies, 2004.

Youth Organizer's Television. *Educational Video. Education Video Handbook. YO-TV Production Handbook. Created by Students for Students*. New York: Education Video Center, 1994.

Web Resources

Adobe Digital Kids Club—www.adobe.com/education/digkids/intro_video
This site provides a comprehensive overview of the pre-production, production, post-production, and distribution of a video.

DV Resources for Beginners—www.dvshop.ca/dvcafe/dv/beginners.html
This site provides a guide to everything from buying a camera to writing a screenplay.

The Internet Movie Database (IMDB)—www.imdb.com
This site is a comprehensive guide to movies and the film industry.

Notes

1. The information from the following section comes from the YO-TV Production Handbook. *Educational Video, Education Video Handbook: YO-TV Production Handbook. Created by Students for Students* (New York: Education Video Center, 1994).

2. The most common video editing method currently used by professionals is through software applications such as "After Effects," "Final Cut Pro," and "iMovie."

CHAPTER TEN

Dance by Kathleen Kingsley, with Case Study by Deborah Reshotko

Dance is one of the oldest and broadest of human activities. In spite of this, or perhaps because of it, dance defies definition. Everyone knows what it is, yet what comes to mind upon hearing the word *dance* is different for everyone. For some, dance means ballet or social dancing. For others, it is a way to tell stories, to express feelings, or to play with design. Whatever the personal or group definition of dance is, it plays a vital role in the expression of human experience, past and present. Movement is considered the architect of the brain[1] and, as such, belongs in schools and community-based settings as an integral part of daily life. The following case study illustrates how SPEAKING OF DANCE, a Colorado-based dance organization, uses dance as a tool for human expression while building community in the urban core of Denver. The chapter ends with a section on the essentials for effectively coordinating dance in a community-art setting, followed by resources for the artistic technique of dance.

SPEAKING OF DANCE Case Study

SPEAKING OF DANCE (SOD) is a dance organization that entertains and educates the public through performances, residencies, and workshops. SOD produces the choreography of its artistic director, Deborah Reshotko, a choreographer interested in exploring concrete subject matter through dance, music, and the spoken word. SOD is committed to using dance as a tool for community outreach and bringing diverse groups of people together—sometimes as performers and sometimes as viewers and participants in discussions about dances that the company performs. The philosophy of SOD is that choreography and performance are vehicles for examining social issues and for celebrating the joy and drama of being human.

The organization's ongoing goal of bringing dance to the community and the community to dance is fulfilled in both community and school settings. In 1998, SOD initiated "Building Community Through Dance," a program in which neighborhood residents of all ages work together to use the art of dance making as a vehicle to enhance community building. The program evolved because SOD was looking for a way to give back to its home community, Capitol Hill, in Denver. The free workshops help bring local children, teens, and adults together and engage them in the artistic process. Through collaboration, the participants create a community of dancers and also learn creative and life skills that they can apply to their everyday lives. Since its inception, more than one thousand adults and children have participated in SOD workshops. Participants include women and families who have recently left the welfare system, students at risk for dropping out of school, children and adults who are new to the United States and speak little English, and longtime Capitol Hill residents of all ages and walks of life.

Program Activities

Building Community Through Dance offers sixteen-week workshops taught by SOD's artistic director and SOD dancers/teachers. The workshops take place in schools and at community organizations from September through November and from January through March. In the workshops, participants learn choreographic techniques and community-building skills that they will apply when they create group dances. In January, there are eight weeks of Saturday morning rehearsals for the final performances. The dances are built around a theme. Themes from past years include "The Neighborhood" (1999), "Mapping Our Lives" (2000), "Transmitting Wisdom Across Generations" (2001), "What is a Family" (2002), "Life Journeys," (2003) and "Opposing Forces: A Search for Peace" (2004). In the rehearsals, children, youth, and adults are brought together from all the program sites to work as a group to choreograph dances for the final performances. The final performances take place in March and are professionally produced by SOD. Local composers are hired to write and perform live music, and lighting designers give the performers the experience of creating and being part of a professional show. This professionalism validates their work and increases their sense of accomplishment. Between 600 and 800 community residents view these free performances annually.

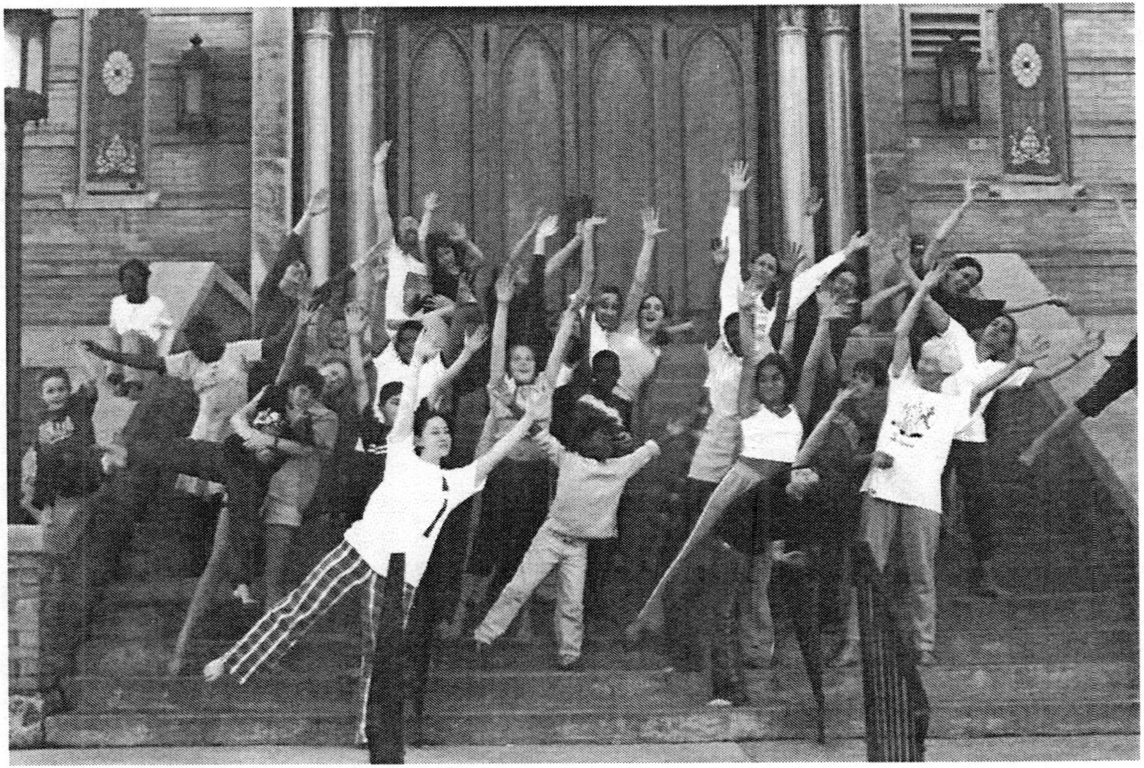

Figure 10.1. ***Building Community Through Dance*** **dancers, SPEAKING OF DANCE, Denver, Colorado.**
Photo credit: Dania Pettus

Essential Elements for Success

Even though Building Community Through Dance has run in a similar fashion for more than six years, the key element for this project is artistic process. It is crucial to have the flexibility to adjust the program yearly, or even weekly, to fit the participants' individual needs and to ensure the highest-quality process and the best final product.

Weekly contact with all project participants is important. When a student (child or adult) misses a workshop, the SOD dancer/teacher calls the student's home. Often, students miss classes because they need rides or because mitigating family circumstances interfere. In many cases, SOD has been able to assist in finding ways for the student to resume his or her attendance, and both children and adults have been very surprised and pleased to receive such assistance. Both groups have commented that this persistence helped them feel cared for and more a part of the community. Some ways SOD has helped participants attend are by finding volunteers to provide transportation for them, feeding participants who came to workshops hungry, and giving dance clothes to participants who had none.

Weekly supervision meetings between the dancers/teachers and the artistic director are also essential to the success of the program. In these meetings, the group processes the specifics of each workshop and discusses ways to help individual participants achieve program goals. In one session in which only sporadic meetings occurred because of schedule conflicts among the dancers/teachers, participants did not progress as successfully overall as in other sessions, thus validating the need for regular supervision meetings.

Developing good contacts in the schools has helped to recruit and retain students. Both the artistic director and program director have meetings with school contacts before beginning a session in a particular school. They outline the responsibilities of both the school and SOD, and ongoing weekly contact with the school helps to build a solid relationship. When students move, lose their phones, or experience crises, SOD staff members can find out more directly and, in some cases, intervene in order to allow the student to continue the workshops.

Even a well-planned and well-executed program needs to change and evolve with time. Sometimes, plans and arrangements that worked fine in the first three years of the program are not as effective in the fourth year. The community changes, and SOD may need to change the program to accommodate the differences observed.

Perhaps the most effective part of the program is its intergenerational nature. Children, teens, and adults are challenged and charmed by each other's imaginations; they are forced to put aside any preconceived notions about

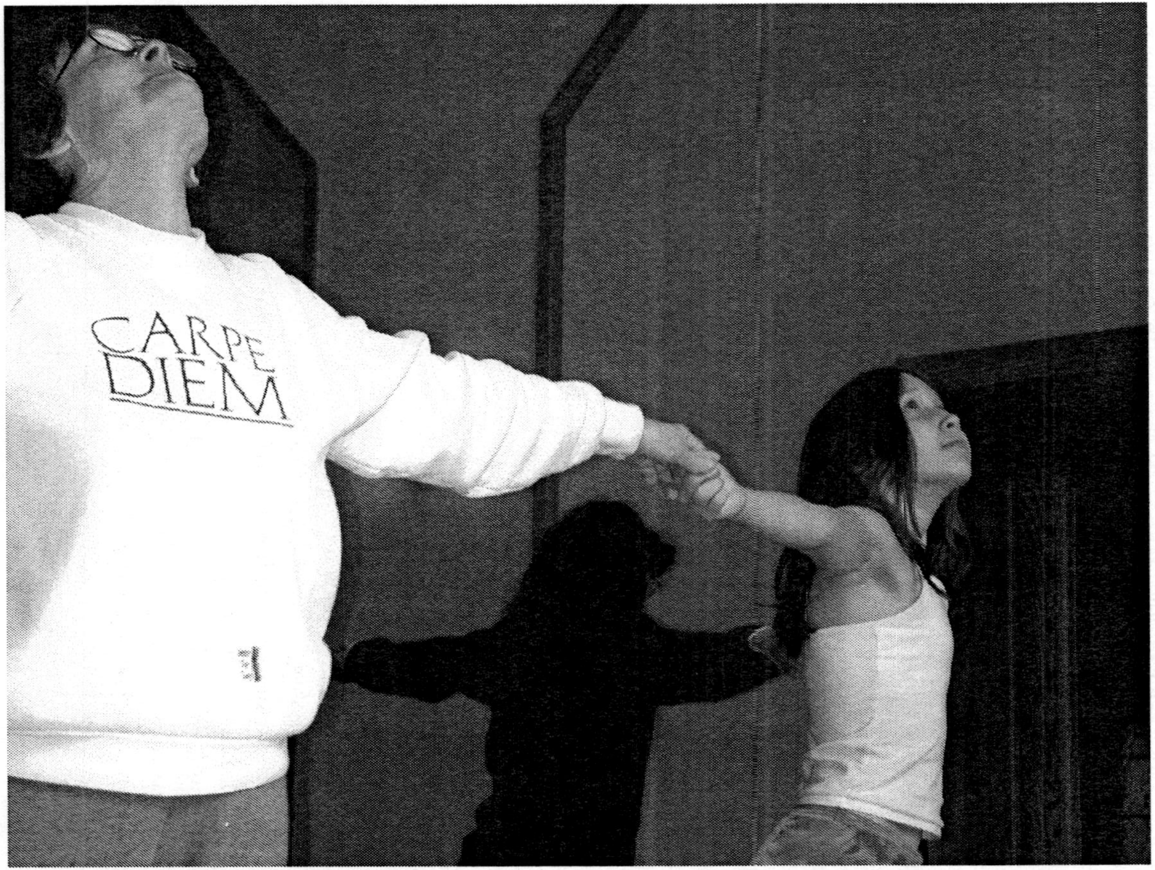

Figure 10.2. ***Building Community Through Dance*** **dancers Kay Obering (l) and Brittany Vicars (r), SPEAKING OF DANCE, Denver, Colorado.**

Photo credit: Greg Cradick

how people of various ages think and act and, eventually, they make friends with one another. The artistic process involves disparate people making a dance together. For example, a fifteen-year-old African-American girl, a nine-year-old Latino boy, and a fifty-five-year-old white woman created a dance about important hurdles that each has overcome, teaching and learning from each other in the process. The age and race categories melted away; instead, there were only three excited imaginations and three moving bodies fueling the process. This part of the work is central to SOD's mission of "bringing dance to the community and the community to dance." It is what ensures that this work will always be fresh, creative, personal, and powerful. The participants use the art of dance to intertwine their diverse life experiences together.

Reflection

The program is evaluated annually in terms of three risk/protective factors that were outlined by the State of Colorado's Department of Public Health and Environment. The factors include increasing commitment to school, inducing pro-social development, and valuing the unique contribution of each individual. The organization's results show that:

- Participants in the program increase their commitment to school and raise their grades: 15 to 18 percent of the participants are placed on their school's honor roll for the first time during their participation with SOD, and there is a 10 percent increase in participants who plan to attend college or post–high school vocational institutions after participating in the program.
- Participants of all ages learn tolerance skills: more than 97 percent report that they are comfortable working with people they had been frightened of or felt were "different" before the workshops.
- Participants report making new friends who are different ages or races or who live in different neighborhoods.
- Because physically and emotionally disabled children and adults are mainstreamed into the program, all participants learn respect for and sensitivity to the differing needs of every individual in the program.
- Children, teens, and adults learn new pro-social skills in the community-building work and in the discipline of rehearsing and performing. At the end of the program, more than 98 percent report that they are able to express themselves better verbally and physically, are much more confident, and have learned to build trust in a diverse group.

The following section provides a brief overview of the essentials for the artistic technique of dance.

Essentials for the Artistic Technique of Dance

Please refer to chapter 2 for an overview of the community-art process that we suggest as a framework. If you are planning a community-based dance project, we strongly recommend collaborating with a professional choreographer or dancer and using the recommended resources to gain an in-depth understanding of the dance process. Below are the essential components, skills, and processes we suggest incorporating into a dance project or program.

Understanding Different Approaches

There are many approaches to integrating dance into a school or community-based setting. Indeed, the definition of dance integration, like the definition of dance, is often a source of confusion. It might help to clarify some differences between *dance education*, *kinesthetic learning*, and *dance integration*.

- *Dance education* is concerned primarily with the history, aesthetics, and techniques of dance as an art form. The National Dance Standards address dance education.
- *Kinesthetic learning* is learning through movement or dance. Children can dance out a multiplication problem through rhythm and beat or through shape of the numbers.
- *Dance integration*, as defined by the Kennedy Center's Partners in Education program, takes place when the student learns about the aesthetics of dance while learning about the subject with which it is being integrated in order to express as much about that subject as possible in aesthetically pleasing dances. In other words, dance integration is beautifully exemplified by the art of choreography or dance composition. When someone creates a dance about the water cycle, he or she is constructing his or her own learning. The dance is also an assessment because the artist practitioner can see quite clearly what the dancer does or does not understand about the water cycle. While all of these approaches to dance in the schools and community are valuable, the dance integration model is the broadest. Dance integration involves learning how to structure dances using the dance elements of body, energy, space, and time. The content, whether scientific, mathematical, or historical, has to be accurate as well as creative. The performance must be focused, and all dancers must know and perform their dance jobs. They must be able to work together for a common goal.

Understanding the Elements of Dance[2]

As participants learn about dance as a means of self-expression and an art form, they should explore and understand the following:

- *The body is the instrument of dance.* Dance students learn to understand the body and to know how to warm the muscles to prevent injuries. They learn that like any athlete, a dancer must understand how to build strength, flexibility, and endurance. Although dancers are athletes, they use their instruments or bodies to express themselves rather than to compete. *Warm-up exercises* build strength, flexibility, and endurance, and they ready the mind and body for dancing. The warm-up is also about building movement vocabulary so that when dancers begin to create, they have a vocabulary of movement and the skills they need.
- Dancers explore the *elements of dance space, time, and energy.*
    - *Space* is the shape of the body with positive and negative space; it is size, levels, directions, facings, and focus. Space is also pathways in space or what it looks like when one travels through space.
    - *Time* is duration; it is rhythm, both metric and breath. Metric rhythm is rhythm that can be counted. It is beat, tempo, recurring rhythm patterns, and accent. Breath rhythm is movement that is not counted. This is the rhythm of the body, like a heartbeat, breath, a tickle, a sneeze, or pain. Breath rhythms exist in nature—for example, the ocean, clouds, wind, snow falling, or leaves twirling and falling.
    - *Energy* is the quality of the movement. It is the force of the movement or the dynamics.
- Dancers understand the *artform and aesthetics of dance.* The elements of space, time, and energy exist together as we move, but dancers explore them individually to bring clarity and articulation to their movement. Simply combining the elements of space, time, and energy to create movement phrases is not dancing. Dance springs from the motional aspects of life's experiences; from one's imagination; and from imagery, abstraction, and metaphor. Dance is the art of motion. When people are concerned with the art of motion, they are concerned with the quality of the act, how a movement takes place, or the manner in which it is carried out.
- Dancers understand the *history and cultural origins of dance* through understanding different genres and forms of music and how they relate to dance. The Virginia Tanner Creative Dance Program (see endnote 2)

uses live musicians so that dancers can learn about music and how music and dance work together to become better dancers. Dancers in the Virginia Tanner Creative Dance Program explore:

- Cultural origins of dance and authentic dances
- Ritual and ceremonial dances
- Different dance genres
- The art form of dance as it exists historically
- Great choreographers and performers through live performances, videos, and demonstrations

Working Collectively

Dance is generally a communal experience, so being able to work together for a common outcome is the norm. Even when a choreographer is working with a group of dancers, it generally is a group effort. We know that some of the most valuable skills we can teach and learn are how to work in groups to problem-solve, how to settle differences, and how to get along. Group choreography is an ideal way to teach these concepts through doing. Groups creating choreography also need reasoning, judgment, and higher-order thinking skills.

Critique is both an important aspect of working collectively and a delicate balance when critiquing peers. It is possible to create an atmosphere of trust within a group of participants that supports careful examination of the works of others in order to help them clarify movement ideas and underlying concepts in a way that is useful, productive, and professional rather than personal. Reflection is an important piece of effective pedagogy. How do you learn? Why did you make the choices that you made in this dance? One of the most valuable lessons school- and community-based educators can provide students is in critical thinking. Creating dances teaches one to think.

Avoiding Risks[3]

- Ensure that the space you have chosen is adequate for full, creative movement, with enough space for students to move freely and safely.
- Be prepared. Have a lesson plan for every class or session and a long-term plan for the semester or project.
- Know your participants. Do they have physical or language limitations? Do they know they are going to move and dance?
- Develop group management skills. When participants are moving, they may be noisy and seemingly out of control. Set signals for quiet, and set physical boundaries to prevent bumping into one another.

Please refer to the following print and web-based resources for more information about the history and technique of dance.

Dance Resources

Case Study Contact Information
SPEAKING OF DANCE
414 Washington Street
Denver, CO 80203
(303) 722-0902
www.speakingofdance.org

Print Resources

Adshead, Janet, and June Layson, eds. *Dance History A Methodology for Study*. London: Dance Books, Ltd., 1983.

Cornett, Claudia. *The Arts as Meaning Makers: Integrating Literature and the Arts Throughout the Curriculum*. Upper Saddle River, N.J.: Prentice-Hall, Inc., 1999.

Croce, Arlene. *Sight Lines*. New York: Alfred A. Knopf, 1987.

Driver, Ian. *A Century of Dance*. London: Octopus Printing Group, 2001.

Gilbert, Anne Green. *Brain-Compatible Dance Education*. Reston, Va.: AAHPERD, 2006.

Gilbert, Anne Green, and Helen Smith. *Creative Dance for All Ages*. Reston, Va.: AAHPERD, 1992.

H'Doubler, Margaret. *Dance: A Creative Experience*. Madison: University of Wisconsin Press, 1998.

Jensen, Eric. *Arts with the Brain in Mind*. Alexandria, Va.: Association for Supervision and Curriculum Development, 2001.

Joyce, Mary. *Dance Technique for Children*. Carmichael, Calif.: Mayfield Publishing Company, 1984.

Joyce, Mary. *First Steps in Teaching Creative Dance to Children*. Mountain View, Calif.: Mayfield Publishing Company, 1994.

Lavender, Larry. *Dancers Talking Dance: Critical Evaluation in the Choreography Class*. Albuquerque: University of New Mexico, 1996.

Lonsdale, Steven. *Animals and the Origins of Dance*. New York: Thames & Hudson, 1982.

Sachs, Curt. *World History of the Dance*. New York: Norton & Company Inc., 1963.

Schrader, Constance. *A Sense of Dance Exploring Your Movement Potential*. Champaign, Ill.: Human Kinetics, 2005.

Web Resources

History of Ballet—www.ccs.neu.edu/home/yiannis/dance/history.html

Kabuki: Basic Information—www.japan-guide.com/e/e2090.html

Foundation for Community Dance—www.communitydance.org.uk

Notes

1. Anne Green Gilbert, *Brain-Compatible Dance Education* (Reston, Va.: AAHPERD, 2006).
2. All information from "Understanding the Elements of Dance" comes from the Utah-based Virginia Tanner Creative Dance Program, a seventy-year-old, nationally and internationally respected nonprofit arts organization that serves more than 13,500 students annually. Through its varied programs and services, such as the Virginia Tanner Studio Program, Children's Dance Theatre, Fine Arts Preschool, Arts-in-Education, Dancers with Disabilities for children and adults, and Professional Development for Educators, the organization nurtures an appreciation of dance, music, literature, theatre, and the visual arts. For more information, visit www.tannerdance.utah.edu.
3. All information from "Avoiding Risks" comes from the Virginia Tanner Creative Dance Program.

APPENDIX A

A Brief History of Murals

Throughout history, peoples all over the earth have created murals to communicate through visual symbols. The cave paintings at Altamira in Northern Spain are some of the earliest-known murals. They were painted around 15,000 B.C. using charcoal, animal fat, and pigment from the earth. During the Italian Renaissance from approximately 1400 to 1550 A.D., the mural was considered the most important form of painting. Artists were commissioned to create murals that illustrated biblical teachings, such as Michelangelo's *Sistine Chapel* and Leonardo da Vinci's *Last Supper*. A significant recent historical evolution of mural making was ushered in by the Mexican Mural Movement.

In 1920, after the Mexican Revolution (1910–1917), the Mexican government initiated a mural program that commissioned artists to create murals to educate and unite the Mexican people. Artists used the fresco technique, which had roots in the pre-Columbian murals of Mexico, to portray imagery. The Mexican Mural Movement influenced artists throughout the world. Many of the artists in the United States who painted murals for the Roosevelt administration's Works Progress Administration (WPA) were influenced by and had connections to the Mexican muralists.

The Civil Rights Movement in the United States (1953–1968) brought with it a period of mural making, whereby murals were created on the grassroots level with the participation of community members. The murals were used as tools for social commentary, for participation in the movement's struggle, and for expressing cultural pride and heritage. For example, a group of

African-American artists started working on *The Wall of Respect* in Chicago in 1967. The *Wall*, which portrayed images of heroic African-American figures, is considered to have catalyzed the contemporary community mural movement in the United States. Mural painting also was an important component of the Chicano Movement. From the early 1960s through the late 1970s and beyond, Chicano and Chicana artists created community-based murals that addressed multiple cultural, social, political, and labor issues, such as those documented by the Social and Public Art Resource Center (SPARC) in its Mexicano/Chicano Mural Database, found on the SPARC website.

Young people's involvement in murals became formalized by the mid-1970s, when governmental entities saw mural making as a positive activity for youth. In the late 1970s, the Carter Administration's Comprehensive Employment and Training Act (CETA) hired artists to create murals, many of which were done in collaboration with young people and school groups. Many cities funded mural programs that involved young people in designing and painting community-based murals. For example, Philadelphia's Mural Arts Program (MAP) began as a graffiti abatement program and has involved the city's youth and adult residents in the creation of more than 2,700 murals since its inception in 1984. The murals are used to create community, recognize the community's heroes, and bring art to the urban landscape.

Chicana muralist Judith F. Baca helped organize and directed the City-Wide Murals Program in Los Angeles in 1974; youth in the program produced more than four hundred murals before the program was disbanded. Baca subsequently co-founded the Social and Public Art Resource Center (SPARC) in 1976 with Christina Schlesinger and Donna Deitch and directed its first mural project—the *Great Wall of Los Angeles*. Baca worked with a diverse group of artists and more than four hundred young people to paint the mural, which documents the history of ethnic peoples of California and spans 2,435 feet of the Tujunga Wash, a flood control channel. SPARC has trained hundreds of youth mural apprentices and worked with thousands of young people during their participatory community murals.

Youth-created murals are varied in contemporary school and community settings. Nonprofit organizations around the country have organized and sponsored numerous mural projects, often in collaboration with schools or local governments. For example, the Chicago Public Art Group has paired artists with community members—often young people—to create high-quality public art pieces. Tim Rollins + K.O.S. (Kids of Survival) is another example of an artist–youth collaboration. Tim, a former special education teacher, has teamed up with young people from the South Bronx to create individual and collective works of art. One piece is the mural *Amerika—For the People of Bathgate*, painted on the side of a Bronx public elementary school and based on Franz Kafka's novel *Amerika*. The composition of the mural consists of horns designed by students and other members of the school community and arranged by Rollins and members of K.O.S. These designs were based on Rollins' request that participants "show your freedom, your individual voice, your spirit in the form of a golden horn."

YouthCity Artways (formerly Global Artways), a Salt Lake City CBAE program, provides affordable, high-caliber introductory arts classes in the visual, musical, and performing arts at neighborhood community centers and libraries. Classes are offered in six-week sessions throughout the school year and summer. Much of the organization's work has involved the production of such murals as *A History of (In)Tolerance* (2004), which is a twenty-four-feet-long by twelve-feet-tall acrylic painting on recycled billboard vinyl that was designed and painted by seventh and eighth graders. During the project, students explored issues of tolerance and intolerance throughout U. S. history, researching heroes of civil rights eras and creating artwork and performances inspired by their research. *A Vibrant Community* (2005) is eight feet long by twelve feet tall. Painted by twenty-five third and fifth graders, the mural shows that people can live together in harmony, no matter what their backgrounds may be. The acrylic image on recycled billboard vinyl displays how diverse backgrounds create a vibrant community.[1] These murals are examples of the numerous projects happening in school and community settings all over the United States and throughout the world.

Note

1. These murals were created with muralist Sarah Moyer.

APPENDIX B

A Brief History of Photography

Sir John Herschel, the British chemist and astronomer who invented a photographic process using sensitized paper, first used the term *photography* in 1839.[1] His work built upon what the Chinese practiced in the fifth century B.C. when they used the technique of *camera obscura*, which is Latin for "dark room." The *camera obscura* originally was a darkened room that admitted light through a small hole in a window covering or wall. Light rays traveling through the hole would reflect the world outside as an inverted image on an internal wall, illustrating an optical law. The camera obscura has been used by many artists, including Michelangelo and Leonardo da Vinci. These artists would trace the image of a person, object, or landscape seen outside the camera obscura. By the 1700s, the camera obscura was made portable by putting it in a box. When a small lens replaced the pinhole, the images became clearer and sharper.

The next important step in the development of photography was the invention of photographic chemicals. These light-sensitive chemicals were needed to make an image permanent. In 1826, the French scientist Joseph Nicéphore Niépce developed the first photograph by placing a plate coated with a chemical inside a camera obscura. Niépce shared his new findings with the artist Louis-Jacques-Mandé Daguerre, who became Niépce's partner. In 1835, two years after Niépce died, Daguerre developed a new process by coating a copper plate with silver oxide in a camera obscura and washing away the excess silver oxide with a solution of water and table salt to prevent the image from darkening over time. In 1839, the *daguerreotype* was announced. The *daguerreotype* took the world by storm and was used widely for portraits. Samuel F. B. Morse, inventor of the telegraph, brought daguerreotypes to the United States, where they were used until the 1850s, long after the European community had switched to the negative/positive photographic process developed by William Henry Fox Talbot. The *calotype* was another photographic invention that was announced in 1841. Talbot, an English inventor, developed the calotype process, which used paper negatives that were saturated with a light-sensitive salt solution. These were called *salted paper prints*.

Another step in the progression of photography was the invention of the *wet collodion process* by English photographer Frederick Scott Archer. Glass negatives were coated with a mixture of potassium iodide and collodion, a transparent, sticky substance that had to be sensitized immediately with a bath of silver nitrate. These glass negatives produced sharper images that lasted longer than paper negatives, and, consequently, more paper prints could be produced from one negative. A similar but less expensive process, called a *tintype*, used an iron plate in place of a glass negative. This process was used widely during the Civil War to photograph soldiers in uniform before going off to battle.

George Eastman invented the first Kodak camera in 1888. In an effort to make photography accessible to many people, in 1900 he introduced the Kodak Brownie box roll-film camera at the price of one dollar. This affordable camera allowed people to take their own photographs without hiring a photographer. The first color film was invented in 1935 by the Eastman Kodak Company.

Most recently, digital photography, which was pioneered by the space program, became available to the public in 1972 with Texas Instruments' filmless camera. In 1981, the first commercial electronic camera—the Mavica—was released by Sony. Today, digital photography is widely used for personal, professional, and educational purposes.

Out of this history came the following types of cameras, which are important to understand when determining project needs.

Types of Cameras

When planning a community photography project, it is important to decide which type of camera to use. This, in part, will determine the developing and printing process. Several different types of cameras are available, depending on skill levels, availability of darkrooms, and duration and depth of the project.

Pinhole Camera

Pinhole cameras are simple cameras that are relatively easy to make.[2] The pinhole camera is a lensless box or cylinder with a pinhole at one end and film or photographic paper at the other. When light is allowed to enter the camera through the pinhole, it falls onto the photographic paper. When the paper is developed, an inverted negative image is created. Pinhole cameras can also use cartridge film, which can be processed at a photo lab. Pinhole images tend to be less sharp than images taken with a lens, and the exposure time of these prints is longer as well.

Disposable Camera

Disposable cameras are inexpensive and have preloaded film as part of the camera. Available in various models, they may have a built-in flash, wide-angle lens, or waterproof capability. Disposable cameras lack a changeable focus, and the inexpensive plastic lens creates images that are not as sharp as point-and-shoot, single-lens reflex, or digital cameras.

Point-and-Shoot Camera

Point-and-shoot cameras are reusable, compact, and easy to use. These cameras may be used without much technical training. Most models have automatic focus and other automatic features. Most have built-in flash and may also have a zoom feature. The viewfinder lens is not the lens that actually takes the picture, which means that the framing of the photograph is not as precise as with a single-lens reflex camera.

Single-Lens Reflex (SLR) Camera

In a single-lens reflex (SLR) camera, the viewfinder lens is the lens that takes the picture, so what one sees through the viewfinder is what appears in the photograph. SLR cameras have interchangeable lenses, and many have separate flash units. They provide the photographer with more opportunities for being creative than with other types of cameras, such as manual and automatic focus options, shutter speed (the speed at which the lens opens and closes) adjustments, and aperture size (the size of the lens opening) modifications.

Digital Camera

Digital cameras are similar to other cameras, but they use digital memory, rather than film, to store photographic images. One can view a digital photograph immediately after taking it, which means that instant decisions may be made about which images to discard, save, or re-shoot. Digital cameras offer different resolutions, which translate to the number of pixels in an image. Higher resolution results in a sharper image. After downloading digital photographs to a Windows or Macintosh computer, one may use numerous software options for editing and printing the images.[3]

Notes

1. The two major sources used for historical and photographic process information are Bonnie Rogers, "The Amazing History of Photography," at historyforkids.utah.gov/fun_and_games/photos/history.html (accessed 1 June 2008) and Museum of Fine Arts, MFA *Boston Gallery Notes: Photography* (Boston: Museum of Fine Arts, 1988).

2. For detailed instructions for making a pinhole camera, see A. Haslam's *Make it Work!: Photography* (please see Photography Resources in Chapter 7).

3. Some of the most popular image editing programs are Adobe's Photoshop and Photoshop Elements, Corel's Corel Photo-Paint, JASC Software's Paint Shop Pro, and Microsoft's PictureIt!

APPENDIX C

A Brief History of Posters and Billboards

Public announcements have been found in the form of inscriptions on Egyptian monuments dating back to the third century B.C. and on the walls of Pompeii, which was destroyed in 79 A.D. In fifteenth-century Europe, most public information was passed on to the people by a town crier, who would walk through the streets and stop at crossroads to announce such important information as proclamations by the king, goods for sale, burials, and special events.

Although there are examples of quasi-commercial public announcements on paper dating as far back as 146 B.C., printed announcements and proclamations did not become common until the invention of the printing press in 1436. The printing press allowed for mass production of posters, making the painstaking process of individually creating proclamations and posters obsolete. The first printed handbill was produced around 1480 by William Caxton.[1] By the mid-1500s, posters had begun to take the place of town criers.

During the sixteenth and seventeenth centuries, most printed notices were from either the church or the state. These official notices—printed with black ink on white paper—announced meetings, public events, and entertainment. In 1791, France passed a law that allowed private individuals to put up posters, but these posters had to be printed on colored paper to differentiate them from official church and state notices.

The invention of *lithography* in 1798 by Alois Senefelder allowed for the mass printing of images on posters. Lithography is a printing process on a smooth surface—originally limestone, but now often metal—on which an image is made using an oil-based medium (ink or crayon). Through a chemical process, a plate is prepared so that the printing ink adheres only to the oil-based crayon or ink marks. Jules Chéret is considered the "father of the poster" and was the first person to mass-produce posters using lithography. Chéret opened a print shop in Paris in 1866, ushering in the age of the poster as an art form. He produced more than one thousand posters during his lifetime. Other notable artists who have created posters include Henri de Toulouse-Lautrec, Alphonse Mucha, Pierre Bonnard, Édouard Manet, Maxfield Parrish, and Leonetto Cappiello.

In 1937, *El Taller de Gráfica Popular* (The Workshop for Popular Graphic Art) was founded in Mexico by a group of artists who wanted to use the print to create social change. This medium of printmaking was ideal because of its visual qualities and reproduction potential. Images could be mass-produced in order to have a wider impact on the populace. The founding artists of El Taller de Gráfica Popular were Leopoldo Méndez, Pablo O'Higgins, and Luis Arenal. They wanted to further the aims of the Mexican Revolution through this medium, as did their contemporaries involved with the Mexican Mural Movement.

In the United States, the graphic arts were used frequently as a tool for social commentary during the 1960s and 1970s. Social movements and war protests used posters as a tool because of their accessibility and low cost. Contemporary billboards and large-scale outdoor posters have arisen from the long, rich history of the poster. Today, we have numerous printmaking and digital graphic capabilities that aid in the creation of posters and billboards.

Note

1. David Bernstein, *Advertising Outdoors: Watch This Space!* (New York: Phaidon, 1997), 12.

APPENDIX D

A Brief History of Video, by Irina Zadov

Although the concept of a video display camera was first introduced in the 1800s,[1] it was not until 1924 that Vladimir Kosma Zworykin invented the first video capture device, known as the *Iconoscope*. Shortly thereafter, Philo Taylor Farnsworth transmitted an image of sixty horizontal lines across a cathode-ray tube. This method was used during the 1936 Berlin Olympics, marking the world's first televised sporting event. Modern analog televisions use this same technique, transmitting electron beams that scan horizontal lines across a cathode-ray tube.

Early television used film rather than video to record monitors in a process called *kinescoping*. In the 1950s, a California-based company, Ampex Electric and Manufacturing Company, created the first modern video recording device that was upgraded to color in 1958. The mid-1970s saw the first analog videocassette recorder used in the private domain. The analog technology created similar, but not identical, recordings. A challenge with analog technology is that the more times the recording is duplicated, the lower the resolution quality will be.

Digital recording, however, does not have this problem. Digital technology is based on the binary digit, or *bit*, which has two states: "on" and "off" (corresponding to one and zero in discrete storage units). Thus, all data found on the Internet, as well as DVDs and CDs, are composed of a sea of ones and zeros. These states may be reproduced identically and do not deteriorate over time. Another benefit of this technology is that it allows for much more compact hardware.

In addition to understanding the technology, deciding which type of video genre to be used is important. Daniel R. Greenwood outlines eight different types of video projects for school-aged children[2] that are relevant to any community-art experience using video. Each of these video genres, outlined below, provides a different type of learning opportunity.

Reality TV

Reality TV is a contemporary mode of production that has been popularized with such shows as *Survivor* and *The Real World*, where nonactors are filmed in various situations with little foreknowledge of what will happen to them or what they are required to do. This is a popular medium because it requires the least amount of preparation. Such elements as scripts, stage directions, and actors are not required. Rather, participants may improvise loosely plotted scenarios to capture the nuances of everyday life. Greenwood suggests that this type of cinematography can be a good educational tool to familiarize participants with the technical aspects of video.

Educational Video

Educational video is another genre widely used in the classroom. Through this method, participants can act as teachers and gain mastery of the subject about which they are speaking. This method is particularly helpful when teaching something that cannot be demonstrated easily in the classroom. The camera can be taken to different locations, and scenes may be reenacted and displayed in ways that are not possible in a regular classroom setting. Another advantage of educational video, when used instead of a presentation, is its ability to address stage fright. Students may create videos in the studio without having to directly face classmates to deliver a speech.

Documentary

Another popular genre is the *documentary* video, which allows participants to delve into a certain topic and represent it honestly and fairly from multiple sides. This approach involves interviewing experts or persons of interest as well as reenacting or narrating certain events. Another important part of the documentary is the use of *establishing shots* and *B-roll*, which puts the narrative into perspective by visually placing it in a time and place. *A-roll* footage, on the other hand, is the interview or narration that guides the story. For instance, if a war veteran is explaining his or her memories of D-Day on the A-roll, the B-roll may be some historical footage from the day.

News Report

A method of telling a story similar to the documentary is a *news report*, which challenges participants to discover what is interesting about a given current or past event and present it in an engaging, imaginative way. This method focuses more than documentaries on public speaking skills. Establishing shots and B-roll will also be important in this genre.

Drama

A familiar type of video on television and in popular film is the *drama*, in which actors play characters and follow a script. This genre allows for participants to develop their acting skills and interact with topics in a creative way. Literature and history can come alive in a classroom setting when participants actively take on the roles they read about in order to understand the subject matter from the characters' points of view. This approach also allows participants to write, direct, and act in their own screenplays while giving them important planning, organizing, and writing skills.

Public Service Announcement

The *public service announcement* is a great way to connect participants with social or environmental issues. Participants can create a message they believe in as they inform others about issues of concern.

Music Video

The *music video* allows participants to develop musical skills and work together to create an audiovisual experience. The set, costumes, and music must be synchronized to create a successful piece. Three primary music video types exist: the performance video, in which participants perform the music; the storyline video, in which participants act out a story to suggest the music; and the montage of images, in which participants create a combination of images that reflect the music.

Video Montage

The final video genre suggested by Greenwood is the *video montage*. This experimental or artistic video includes a combination of various images to create a message or explore the interaction of various ideas. Video montages may be quite imaginative and elaborate. They may also be straightforward or commercial. Participants decide what message to portray using imagery and which sound or words (if any) should accompany the imagery.

Notes

1. The historical part of this chapter stems from Deras Flynn's research in his *Guide to Creating Digital Video Like a Pro* (San Francisco: Que Series TechTV, 2002).
2. Daniel R. Greenwood, *Action! In the Classroom: A Guide to Student Produced Digital Video in K–12 Education* (Oxford, U.K.: The Scarecrow Press, Inc., 2003).

APPENDIX E

A Brief History of Dance

The roots of dance, like the roots of music and drama, reach back to the earliest peoples. Before there were words to communicate, we had movement. There is evidence that language in the beginning was gesture based. Words came much later as shorthand for movement. We moved to express our emotions, desires, hopes, and fears. We danced about our place in the cosmos. Sometimes that movement was to communicate with other people, and sometimes it was a form of communication between the dancer and the universe. These are the origins of both ritual dance and social dance.

Ritual Dance

Ritual dance, rooted in human expression, spirit, and soul, still concerns itself with the balance and alignment of the natural world and our place in it. It recognizes our needs as humans to survive against the larger background of our environment. Rituals of tension (or asking), such as rain dances or hunting dances, and rituals of release (or thanksgiving) require the dancers to become vessels for the spirits of their people in order to communicate with the powers that be. For example, in puebloan ceremonial dances, all tribe members are part of the dance, whether they actually dance or not, because they hold the prayer in their hearts. Puebloan peoples have kachinas, or elemental/ancestral beings, who dance to educate tribal members about their cosmology, history, science, and inter/intrapersonal interactions. Aboriginals use myth to teach how unnecessary or careless actions bring about catastrophe in the world. Connected to long-term observations of the natural world, tribal art and dance is a public and ever-renewed mnemonic, and its patterns and designs have educational as well as sacred functions.

As humans developed articulated spiritual beliefs, dancing moved into the temples and other places of worship. Through developing a more codified movement, these dances became a way to keep a culture alive by telling stories through specific movements. For example, Bharatanatyam, a classical East Indian dance form performed today as entertainment, was once performed by temple dancers to teach people the cosmology of Hinduism.

The Catholic Church played a significant role in affecting attitudes toward dance in Western Europe. The advent of Christianity tended to downplay the highly revered role dance had held in spiritual practices. With the belief that all things of the body were low and devil-like and all things of the mind were higher to heaven and more spiritual, dance was moved out of places of worship. Thus began its decent into an association with more plebeian purposes. As a result of this schism, Europeans, and, by extension, Americans, suffered a break in the unity of body and mind that to this day permeates American culture.

Social Dance

Social dance, or folk dance, is a second area of dance and also rich in historical, sociological, and cultural study. Although often rooted in ritual dance, folk dancing has lost most, if not all, of its original ritual aspects. For example, such European folk dances as Maypole dances have their origins in pagan rituals. Often, social dance styles reflected a highly structured and rigid class system, such as those in Medieval and Renaissance Europe. The dances of the royal courts were extremely formal and refined. By the mid-nineteenth century and the age of Romanticism, the rise of the Viennese waltzes swept Europe's royalty.

Often social dance movements find their origins in simple, everyday actions. In Brazil, the samba, once an African ancestral spirit dance, transformed into a social dance and the country's unofficial national dance. Folk dances in Ireland, based on the fast rhythms of the spinning wheel, became today's Irish jigs and fast-patterned foot dances. At the turn of the century in America's rural south, the dances of black sharecroppers frequently were based on such ordinary movements as milking the cow, picking cotton, or rocking the baby to sleep. As African-Americans steadily moved north, these dance movements went with them, changing in range and intent with the move to more industrial areas.

Theatrical Dance

In the sixteenth century, King Louis XIV of France spearheaded the refinement of dance to such an extent that the best dancers began to perform for the other, less-talented members of the court. The idea that some people could, by virtue of practice, develop a movement technique for the sole purpose of entertaining an elite group of social peers who could not was a new idea in Europe. This was the birth of ballet as descendants of Western culture know it. Theatrical dance, then, is the third great branch of dance. Like ritual and social dance, the edges are not always clearly defined, and the intent of the dance, rather than the content, may help define it. But there will always be dances on the cusp that defy any classification. Dance, if nothing else, is always in motion.

Conceptualizing dance as entertainment has played a large role in the development of the American dance scene. A movement of "serious" theatrical dance closely paralleled the rise of vaudeville and then Broadway. At the end of the nineteenth and beginning of the twentieth centuries, dance companies from Europe introduced ballet to the largest American cities. At about this same time, a truly American revolution in dance was spearheaded by Isadora Duncan. Isadora, tired of swans and princes, tutus and point shoes, threw off the shackles of European ballet. Returning to the Western civilization of the Greeks, she donned white robes and danced barefoot to music of Bach and Beethoven in order to express ideas of freedom, brotherhood, and equality. This was the first time in America that dance became, for some members of the dominant white culture, a vehicle to express spirit and soul. Very soon, schools of dance opened up across America where little girls dressed in white robes (the Isadorables) could express themselves through dance.

Isadora was an iconoclast. Her ideas spawned the American modern dance movement. Ruth St. Denis and Ted Shawn, who together formed the Denishawn School of Dancing and Related Arts in Los Angeles, quickly followed her. Here students studied folk and religious dances from all over the world as well as music composition and drama. Students at this school included Martha Graham, Doris Humphrey, and Charles Weidman, all of whom composed the next generation of prominent modern dancers.

By the 1930s and 1940s, the Martha Graham Dance Company and the Humphrey–Weidman Company were well established, with recognized dance techniques. Martha explored the relationship of core and distal edge. Her movement initiated deep in the body's center, the solar plexus, and expanded sequentially out to feet and hands. Sharp, jagged, and explosive movements with very clear shapes etched her choreography. Her dances were visionary, primal, and soulful. Doris, meanwhile, was exploring the effects of gravity on the human body. Her technique was one of fall and recovery, weight and momentum. Her dances were compositional wonders of visual and movement design that captured her audiences and made them feel as if they, too, were dancing.

The 1930s and 1940s were a time of upheaval of political thought in America and in the rest of the world. The times were reflected in the choreographic choices of many dancers. Dances were no longer about European fairy tales: they were not abstract designs as much as they were expressions of passion and social conscience.

Of important note here, however, is that the dancers expressing these thoughts were mostly white, as the United States was still a segregated society. Black dance in America had its own evolutionary path. From the rural south to the vaudeville stage, black dancers struggled for the same equality white dancers were dancing about. The roots of American dance that are grounded in the African-American culture and experience are vast. Drums, rhythm, syncopation, isolation of body parts while moving, tap dancing, soft shoe, popular dances from the 1920s through the 1940s, vaudeville, and later Broadway owe nearly everything to black dance. Such dancers as Pearl Primus, Katherine Dunham, Talley Beatty, and Alvin Ailey brought heart, soul, earth, and color to the modern dance lexicon.

With the arrival of George Balanchine from Russia and the establishment of the New York City Ballet, a uniquely American style of ballet was born. By the 1960s, the explosion of American theatrical dance was truly remarkable. Paul Taylor, José Limón, Erick Hawkins, Merce Cunningham, Twyla Tharp, Alwin Nikolais, Murray Louis, and Louis Falco, among many others, had joined Martha and Doris. American dance had arrived.

During the 1970s, dance artists began to visit public schools to demystify the art form for students; this initiated the federally funded artist in education programs. Although the original idea behind these programs was to share the dancers' art and vision with students, the emphasis shifted from the artist in education to arts in education. The working dancer/choreographer sharing with students his or her passion about the art form morphed into the teaching artist, knowledgeable about pedagogical practices and able to integrate his or her art form into the fabric of the school's learning environment.

This shift from visiting dancer to dance teaching artist is an important one. Brain research tells us that young people need to be physically active. Our brains rely on a specific sequence of developmental movement patterns to grow dendrites and axons. Movement literally grows a functioning brain and nervous system. Every human baby, if allowed "tummy time," will automatically go through these developmental patterns that are genetically hardwired in us. In fact, there is evidence that if this patterning process suffers interference, a child can present sensory–motor, emotional, and attention gaps.

Dance educator Anne Green Gilbert states that movement is the architect of the brain.[1] Dance belongs in the schools and in community-based settings—not only as an exotic art form shared by a professional dancer on the occasional visit but also as an integral part of daily teaching and learning.

Some School-Based Examples

At Rio Gallinas Charter School for Ecology and the Arts in Las Vegas, New Mexico, all students dance, taking classes in creative movement, choreography, jazz, and Afro-Brazilian dance. Rio Gallinas is an expeditionary learning school, so all subjects are integrated through in-depth investigations or "expeditions" about a certain topic. Dance and visual art are part of that integration. In the expedition "Following the Footsteps of the Hermit," the learning journey focused on the hermit Giovanni Agostini, who lived in a cave near Las Vegas in 1863. The children discovered stories about him, which they wrote into a marionette show. They created characters from the village of Gallinas in 1863 and wrote diaries using the voices of those characters. Then they created monologues, dialogues, and dances based on what kinds of work would have been done in the village of Gallinas during each season. The culminating dances were simple, honest, and clear and spoke volumes about what the children knew of life in the village of Gallinas; when they performed these dances, the audience was moved to tears.

Another example of using dance in the school is a series of "movement challenges" given to students in a Springfield, Ohio, public school. One group of three students was assigned to show in movement how two tributaries can join a main river as it flows to the ocean. The students could add any elements they wanted to the dance, such as fish, boats, and waterfalls, as long as they showed this challenge. They also were required to have a beginning shape and an ending shape. In the performance, the three students positioned themselves in three different spots in the school gymnasium. They then wound their way to the center of the gym and proceeded to walk in a large circle for a few seconds before collapsing in a heap on the floor. The students later explained that the heap represented a waterfall, but they could not explain the circle they had made in their walk. After further discussion, they decided that layering their bodies on the floor would have created a more visually exciting ending, as it would capture the moment the water falls over the edge and is pulled by gravity, thus capturing a moment in time. The students did not meet their challenge of showing the junction of tributaries with a river, however, and when asked about this, they said they did not know what a river or a tributary was. Although the teacher moaned that they had "learned" those concepts earlier, it was clear that these children had never seen a river and therefore had no schema to be able to show one in movement.

The challenge for artists is to create memorable art that reintegrates the art form with knowledge of who we are. The challenge to dance educators is to teach truths about the natural world and our place in it and to empower others to create meaningful, artistic dances—to create truth as well as beauty. Dance as ritual, education, expression, theater, technique, language of gesture, and a way to develop and enhance cognition must have a place in our society in the twenty-first century.

Note

1. Anne Green Gilbert, *Brain-Compatible Dance Education* (Reston, Va.: AAHPERD, 2006).

APPENDIX F

General Resources

Community Art, Community-Based Art Education, and Community Cultural Development

Binns, Vivienne. *Community and the Arts: History, Theory, Practice.* Leichhardt, New South Wales, Australia: Pluto Press, 1991.

Blandy, Doug, Kristin Congdon, and Paul Bolin, eds. *Histories of Community Based Art Education.* Reston, Va.: National Art Education Association, 2001.

Cleveland, William. *Art in Other Places: Artists at Work in America's Community and Social Institutions.* Westport, Conn.: Praeger Publications, 2000/1987.

Congdon, Kristin. *Community Art in Action.* Worcester, Mass.: Davis Publications, Inc., 2004.

Dreeszen, Craig. *Intersections II: Community Arts and Education Collaborations.* Amherst: Arts Extension Service, 1991.

Elizabeth, Lynne, and Suzanne Young, eds. *Works of Heart: Building Village Through the Arts.* Oakland, Calif.: New Village Press, 2006.

Farnum, Marlene, and Rebecca Schaffer. *YouthARTS Handbook: Art Programs for Youth at Risk.* Washington, D.C.: Americans for the Arts, 1998.

Goldbard, Arlene. *New Creative Community: The Art of Cultural Development.* Oakland, Calif.: New Village Press, 2006.

Hillman, Grady, and Katherine Gaffney. *Training Artists to Work in Alternative Settings.* Washington, D.C.: Americans for the Arts, 1997.

Irwin, Rita, and Anna Kindler, eds. *Beyond the School: Community and Institutional Partnerships in Art Education*. Reston, Va.: National Art Education Association, 1999.

Korza, Pam, and Barbara Schaffer Bacon. *Art, Dialogue, Action, Activism: Case Studies from Animating Democracy*. Washington, D.C.: Americans for the Arts, 2005.

Korza, Pam, Barbara Schaffer Bacon, and Andrea Assaf. *Civic Dialogue, Arts & Culture: Findings from Animating Democracy*. Washington, D.C.: Americans for the Arts, 2005.

London, Peter. *Step Outside: Community-Based Art Education*. Portsmouth, N.H.: Heinemann, 1994.

Klein, Deborah. *Artists & Communities: America Creates for the New Millennium*. Baltimore, Md.: Mid Atlantic Arts Foundation, 2003.

Remer, Jane. *Beyond Enrichment: Building Effective Arts Partnerships with Schools and Your Community*. New York: American Council for the Arts, 1996.

Schwarzman, Matt and Knight, Keith. *Beginner's Guide to Community-Based Arts*. Oakland, CA: New Village Press, 2005.

Web Resources

Chicago Public Art Group—www.cpag.net/home
Community Arts Network—www.communityarts.net
Kennedy Center ArtsEdge—artsedge.kennedy-center.org
National Art Education Association—www.naea-reston.org

Community Art Centers and Programs in Higher Education

Arts of Citizenship Program, University of Michigan
1024 Hill Street
Ann Arbor, MI 48104-3310
(734) 647-7402
www.umich.edu/~mserve/artsofcitizenship

ArtsBridge America
www.artsbridgeamerica.com

Center for Art and Community Partnerships, Massachusetts College of Art and Design
621 Huntington Avenue
Boston, MA 02115
(617) 879-7331
www.massart.edu/partnerships

Center for Art and Public Life, California College of the Arts
5212 Broadway
Oakland, CA 94618
(510) 594-3763
center.cca.edu

Haas Center for Public Service
562 Salvatierra Walk
Stanford, CA 94305-8620
(650) 723-0992
haas.stanford.edu

Institute for Art and Civic Engagement, School of the Museum of Fine Arts, Boston
230 The Fenway
Boston, MA 02115
(617) 267-6100
www.smfa.edu

LINKING Service-Learning and the Arts Program, California State University
www.calstate.edu/csl/initiatives/link_getty.shtml

P.L.A.C.E. Program (Partnership Learning through Art, Culture & the Environment), University of New Mexico
College of Fine Arts
MSC04 2570 (Room 1103)
1 University of New Mexico
Albuquerque, NM 87131-0001
(505) 277-6574
place.unm.edu

SmART (Saturday Morning Art Program), Rowan University
Art Department, Westby Hall
201 Mullica Hill Road
Glassboro, NJ 08028
(856) 256-4520
www.rowan.edu/college/fpa/smart

Spiral Workshop Art Education Program, University of Illinois at Chicago
(312) 996-3337
www.uic.edu/classes/ad/ad382/sites/SpiralWorkshop/SW_index.html

Stanford Institute for Diversity in the Arts
375 Santa Teresa #5
Stanford, CA 94305-8620
(650) 724-3657
www.stanford.edu/dept/ida

Community Building

Kagan, Spencer. *Cooperative Learning*. San Clemente, Calif.: Kagan Cooperative Learning, 1997.

Kretzmann, John P. and John L. McKnight. *Building Communities from the Inside Out: A Path Toward Finding and Mobilizing a Community's Assets*. Evanston, Ill.: Institute for Policy Research, 1993.

Rohnke, Karl. *Funn 'n Games*. Dubuque, Iowa: Kendall/Hunt Publishing Co., 2004.

Facilitation

Kaner, Sam. *Facilitator's Guide to Participatory Decision-Making*. San Francisco: Jossey-Bass, 2007.

Funding

Foundation Center—www.foundationcenter.org
Council on Foundations—www.cof.org
Foundations On-Line—www.foundations.org
Grants.gov—www.grants.gov
Grassroots Fundraising Journal—www.grassrootsfundraising.org
Grant Writing USA—www.grantwritingusa.com

Legal

Volunteer Lawyers for the Arts
www.vlany.org

Strategic Questioning

Peavey, Fran. "Strategic Questioning," in Greene, Tova, Peter Woodrow, and Fran Peavey, *Insight and Action: How to Discover and Support a Life of Integrity and Commitment to Change* (Gabriola Island, British Columbia: New Society Publishers, 1994).

Bibliography

Ancona, George. *Murals: Walls That Sing.* New York: Marshall Cavendish Corp., 2003.

Barber, Benjamin. *An Aristocracy of Everyone: The Politics of Education and the Future of America.* Oxford, New York, and Toronto: Oxford University Press, 1992.

Becker, Howard S. *Art Worlds.* Berkeley: University of California Press, 1982.

Begley, Sharon. "Your Child's Brain." *Newsweek,* February 19, 1996, 55–62.

Bernstein, David. *Advertising Outdoors: Watch This Space!* New York: Phaidon, 1997.

Boal, Augusto. *The Rainbow of Desire.* New York: Routledge, 1995.

Bourdieu, Pierre. *The Field of Cultural Production.* New York: Columbia University Press, 1993.

Brown II, Edward. "Community-Based Art in Philadelphia." *Art Papers* 18, no. 3 (May–June 1994): 38–40.

Burton, Judith, Robert Horowitz, and Hal Abeles. "Learning in and through the Arts: Curricular Implications." In *Champions of Change: The Impact of the Arts on Learning,* edited by Edward B. Fiske, 35–46. Washington, D.C.: The Arts Education Partnership and the President's Committee on the Arts and Humanities, 1999.

Catterall, James S. "Involvement in the Arts and Success in Secondary School." *Americans for the Arts Monograph Series* 1, no. 9 (December 1997/January 1998).

Catterall, James S., Richard Chapleau, and John Iwanaga. "Involvement in the Arts and Human Development: General Involvement and Intense Involvement in Music and Theatre Arts." In *Champions of Change: The Impact of the Arts on Learning,* edited by Edward B. Fiske, 1–18. Washington, D.C.: The Arts Education Partnership and the President's Committee on the Arts and Humanities, 1999.

Cohen, Anthony. *The Symbolic Construction of Community.* New York: Tavistock Publications, 1985.

Congdon, Kristin, Doug Blandy, and Paul Bolin. *Histories of Community-Based Art Education*. Reston, Va.: National Art Education Association, 2001.

Costello, Laura. *Part of the Solution: Creative Alternatives for Youth*. Washington, D.C.: National Assembly of State Arts Agencies, 1995.

Cyphert, Dale, "Pleasure, Pedagogy, and Oppression in the Heartland." *Text and Performance Quarterly* 18, no. 1 (1998): 37–49.

Davidson, Ann Locke. *Making and Molding Identity in Schools: Student Narratives on Race, Gender, and Academic Engagement*. Albany: SUNY Press, 1996.

Dewey, John. *Art as Experience*. New York: Minton, Balch & Company, 1934.

Dickson, Malcolm. *Art With People*. Sunderland, England: AN Publications, 1995.

Dissanayake, Ellen. *Homo Aestheticus*. New York: The Free Press, 1992.

Duddy, Tom. "The Politics of Creativity." *CIRCA* Vol. 68 (Summer 1994): 28–31.

Ewald, Wendy. *Peace and Harmony: Carver Portraits*. New York: Distributed Art Publishers, 2006.

Ewald, Wendy, and Alexandra Lightfoot. *I Wanna Take Me a Picture: Teaching Photography and Writing to Children*. Durham, N.C.: Center for Documentary Studies, 2001.

Ewald, Wendy, and Louise Neri, eds. *Towards a Promised Land*. London: Steidl Publishing, 2006.

Ewell, Maryo. "Some Historical Threads of the Community Arts Story (and Why They Are Important)," July 2001. Available at www.communityarts.net/readingroom/archivefiles/2002/07/some_historical.php (accessed June 1, 2008).

Ewell, Maryo, and Peter Ewell. "Planning for Grassroots Arts Development." *Arts in Society* 12, no. 1 (Summer 1975): 92–109.

Felshin, Nina, ed. *But Is It Art? The Spirit of Art as Activism*. Seattle: Bay Press, Inc., 1995.

Fisher, David. "Public Art and Public Space." *Soundings* 79, no. 1–2 (Spring–Summer 1996): 41–57.

Flood, W. "Animation: Socio-cultural Community Development in Europe and the United States." Ph.D. diss., Pennsylvania State University, 1982.

Flynn, Deras. *Guide to Creating Digital Video Like a Pro*. San Francisco: Que Series TechTV, 2002.

Fromm, Erich. *The Sane Society*. New York: Holt, Rinehart & Winston, 1955.

Gecas, Viktor. "The Social Psychology of Self-Efficacy." *Annual Review of Sociology* 15 (August 1989): 291–316.

Gilbert, Anne Green. *Brain-Compatible Dance Education*. Reston, Va.: AAHPERD, 2006.

Goffman, Erving. *The Presentation of Self in Everyday Life*. Garden City, N.Y.: Doubleday and Company, Inc., 1959.

Goldbard, Arlene. *New Creative Community: The Art of Cultural Development*. Oakland, Calif.: New Village Press, 2006.

Goldbard, Arlene. "Postscript to the Past: Notes Toward a History of Community Arts." *High Performance* 16, no. 4 (Winter 1993): 23–27.

Golden, Jane, Robin Rice, and Monica Yant Kinney. *Philadelphia Murals and the Stories They Tell.* Philadelphia: Temple University Press, 2002.

Greene, Maxine. *Releasing the Imagination: Essays on Education, the Arts, and Social Change.* San Francisco: Jossey-Bass, 1995.

Greene, Tova, Peter Woodrow, and Fran Peavey. *Insight and Action: How to Discover and Support a Life of Integrity and Commitment to Change.* Gabriola Island, B.C.: New Society Publishers, 1994.

Greenwood, Daniel, R. *Action! In the Classroom: A Guide to Student Produced Digital Video in K–12 Education.* Oxford, U.K.: The Scarecrow Press, Inc., 2003.

Gude, Olivia. "Beyond Monological Monuments: The Possibility of Heteroglossia in Public Space." *Public Art Review*, no. 12 (Spring/Summer 1995): 40.

Hawkin, Gay. *From Nimbin to Mardi Gras: Constructing Community Arts.* Melbourne, Australia: Allen & Unwin, 1993.

Heath, Shirley Brice, and Adelma Roach. "Imaginative Activity: Learning in the Arts During the Non-School Hours." In *Champions of Change: The Impact of the Arts on Learning*, edited by E. B. Fiske, 20–34. Washington, D.C.: The Arts Education Partnership and the President's Committee on the Arts and Humanities, 1999.

Heath, Shirley Brice, Elisabeth Soep, and Adelma Roach. "Living the Arts through Language and Learning: A Report on Community-Based Youth Organizations." *Americans for the Arts Monographs* 2, no. 7 (November 1998): 1–20.

Heath, Shirley Brice, and Milbrey McLaughlin, eds. *Identity and Inner-City Youth: Beyond Ethnicity and Gender.* New York: Teachers College Press, 1993.

Holloway, Debra, and Beth Krensky. "The Arts, Urban Education, and Social Change." *Education and Urban Society* 33, no. 4 (August 2001): 354–65.

Holloway, Debra L., and Margaret D. LeCompte. "Becoming Somebody!: How Arts Programs Support Positive Identity for Middle School Girls." *Education and Urban Society* 33, no. 4 (August 2001): 388–408.

Jones, Bernie. "The Community Artist as Community Development Catalyst: An Evaluation of a Pilot Project." *Journal of the Community Development Society* 19, no. 1 (1988): 37–50.

Kaner, Sam. *Facilitator's Guide to Participatory Decision-Making.* San Francisco: Jossey-Bass, 2007.

Krensky, Beth. "An Act of Hope: Developing Social Responsibility through Issue-Oriented Community-Based Art Education." Ph.D. diss., University of Colorado, Boulder, 2002.

Krensky, Beth. "Going Beyond Zebra: A Middle School and Community-Based Arts Organization Collaborate for Change." *Education and Urban Society* 33, no. 4 (August 2001): 427–44.

Krensky, Beth, and Debra L. Holloway, eds. *Education and Urban Society Special Issue: The Arts, Urban Education, and Social Change* 33, no. 4 (August 2001).

Krensky, Beth, with Neal Boyle, Roselyn Boyle, Patrick Gould, and Christian Rodriguez. *A Piece of Peace: Kids Share Their Lives through Poetry, Art & Photography.* Newton, Mass.: Font & Center Press, 1995.

Kretzmann, John P., and John L McKnight. *Building Communities from the Inside Out: A Path Toward Finding and Mobilizing a Community's Assets*. Evanston, Ill.: Institute for Policy Research, 1993.

Landa, Robin. *Graphic Design Solutions*. Albany: On Word Press, 2001.

Lewandowsky, Pina, and Francis Zeischegg. *A Practical Guide to Digital Design: Designing With Your Computer Made Easy!* Lausanne, Switzerland: AVA Publishing SA, 2003.

Lowe, Seana. "The Art of Community Development." Ph.D. diss., University of Colorado, Boulder, 2002.

Lowe, Seana. "The Art of Community Transformation." *Education and Urban Society* 33, no. 4 (August 2001): 457–71.

Lowe, Seana. "Creating Community: Art for Community Development." *Journal of Contemporary Ethnography* 29, no. 3 (June 2000): 357–86.

Mahony, E. "Once Is Too Much." *Art Bulletin* (April/May1998): 17–18.

Marché, Theresa. "Looking Outward, Looking in: Community in Art Education." *Art Education* 51, no. 3 (May 1998): 6–13.

Martinez, Valerie Kim. *Working Draft: Mural Design and Technique*. Salt Lake City: University of Utah, 2006.

McFee, June King. "Change and the Cultural Dimensions of Art Education." In *Context, Content, and Community in Art Education: Beyond Postmodernism*, edited by Ronald N. Neperud, 171–92. New York: Teachers College Press, 1995.

MFA *Boston Gallery Notes: Photography*. Boston: Museum of Fine Arts, 1988.

National Art Education Association. "Where's the Art?" *National Art Education Association*. 2006. Available at www.naea-reston.org/news_advocacy_15flyers.html (accessed September 1, 2006).

Oldenburg, Ray. *The Great Good Places: Cafés, Coffee Shops, Community Centers, Beauty Parlors, General Stores, Bars, Hang Outs, and How They Get You Through the Day*. New York: Paragon, 1989.

Overton, P. "Arts Development in Rural and Small Towns." *Connections Quarterly* (Winter 1987): 12ff.

Pacific, Robin. "This Is Not a Benetton Ad: The Theory of Community Art." *MIX* 23, no. 3 (Winter 1997–1998): 40–43.

Perlstein, Susan. "Intergenerational Arts: Cultural Continuity and Community Cohesion." *Journal of Aging and Identity* 2, no. 4 (1997): 273–284.

Puleo, Mev. "Art as Advocacy." *Breakthrough* (Winter/Summer 1990): 25.

Purpel, David E. *The Moral and Spiritual Crisis in Education: A Curriculum for Justice and Compassion in Education*. New York; Westport, Conn.; and London: Bergin and Garvey, 1989.

Raven, Arlene. *Art in the Public Interest*. New York: Da Capo Press, 1993.

Rogers, Bonnie. "The Amazing History of Photography." Available at historyforkids.utah.gov/fun_and_games/photos/history.html (accessed June 1, 2008).

Rogoff, Barbara. "Developing Understanding of the Idea of Communities of Learners." *Mind, Culture, and Activity* 1, no. 4 (1994): 222.

Rogoff, Barbara. "Evaluating Development in the Process of Participation: Theory, Methods, and Practice Building on Each Other." Draft chapter for *Change and Development: Issues of Theory, Application, and Method,* edited by E. Amsel and A. Renninger. Hillsdale, N.J.: Erlbaum, 1995, 2.

Rohnke, Karl. *Funn 'n Games*. Dubuque, Iowa: Kendall/Hunt Publishing Co., 2004.

Shin, Seung-Ruyl, and Marilyn Proctor. "Teaching Computer Graphic Design." *National Art Education Association Advisory* (Summer 2005): 1.

Shreeve, James. "Music of the Hemispheres." *Discover*, October 1996, 90–100.

Simmons III, Seymour. "Creating Community through Art: Two Research Project Reviews." *The Journal of Social Theory in Art Education*, no. 18 (1998): 59–76.

Stanzioloa, Javier. *Arts, Government and Community Revitalization*. Sydney: Ashgate, 1999.

Van Erven, Eugene. *Community Theatre: Global Perspectives*. New York: Routledge, 2001.

Varnedoe, Kurt, and Blake Gopnick. *Modern Art and Popular Culture: Readings in High and Low*. New York: Harry N. Abrams, 1990.

Vidich, Arthur, and Joseph Bensman. *Small Town in Mass Society*. Princeton: Princeton University Press, 1968.

Vygotsky, Lev S. *The Psychology of Art*. Cambridge, Mass.: The MIT Press, 1925/1971.

Vygotsky, Lev S. *Thought and Language*. Cambridge, Mass.: The MIT Press, 1934/1962.

Vygotsky, Lev S., with Michael Cole, Vera John-Steiner, Sylvia Scribner, and Ellen Souberman, eds. *Mind in Society: The Development of Higher Psychological Processes*. Cambridge, Mass.: Harvard University Press, 1978.

Weitz, Judith H. *Coming Up Taller: Arts and Humanities Programs for Children and Youth at Risk*. Washington, D.C.: President's Committee on the Arts and the Humanities, 1996.

Williams, Robin. *The Non-Designer's Design Book, Third Edition*. Berkeley: Peachpit Press, 2005.

Wositzky, Helen. "Out of the Ashes, a Community Responds: The Dandenong Ranges Bushfires." *Australian Journal of Emergency Management* (Winter 1998): 17–20.

Youth Organizer's Television. *Educational Video. Education Video Handbook. YO-TV Production Handbook. Created by Students for Students*. New York: Education Video Center, 1994.

Index

Numbers in italics refer to figures, tables, and illustrations.

About the Authors

Beth Krensky is an assistant professor of art education and the Area Head of Art Teaching at the University of Utah. She is an artist, activist, and educator. She received a BFA from the Boston Museum School, a master's degree from the Harvard Graduate School of Education, and a PhD in Educational Foundations, Policy, and Practice from the University of Colorado at Boulder, where she wrote her dissertation about the connections between youth-created activist art and social responsibility. Her current research interests include collaborative activist art, arts-based service learning, and civic engagement. She has exhibited widely throughout the United States and internationally. She is a founding member of Artnauts, an international artist collective. She co-founded and spent a decade as co-executive director of the youth arts/service/action organization Project YES (Youth Envisioning Social change). She has coordinated numerous public art initiatives with young artists throughout the United States. She has received multiple honors and awards for her teaching, scholarship, and art.

Seana Lowe Steffen is the founding executive director of the Transformative Leadership Institute and an instructional guide with Mapleton Public Schools, Colorado. Prior to that, she was the founding director of INVST Community Studies at the University of Colorado at Boulder. Dr. Steffen received her PhD in Sociology from the University of Colorado and Bachelor of Arts degrees in Psychology and French from Denison University. In addition, she was a Fellow at the University of Chicago Graduate School of Business. Her research interests are participatory education, community development, responsible business leadership, and social change. In the private and nonprofit sectors, Dr. Steffen brings her expertise to strategic consulting, executive coaching, and capacity building. She is a founding member of Explore Elementary Expeditionary Learning School and also co-founded the Rocky Mountain Youth Corps. Among her awards for leadership and teaching, she most recently received the E-chievement Award for making a lasting difference in the community and beyond. Her website is EngageThroughArt.org.